The Road to Purpose

All rights reserved. No part of this publication may be reproduced or transmitted in any form or by any means, electronic or mechanical, including photocopying, recording, or by any information storage and retrieval system, without the prior written permission from the author, except where permitted by law. Contact the author information on foreign rights.

Printed in the United States of America

Copyright © 2019 Carine Dorlus

ISBN: 978-0-578-49984-0

Book cover design: DeLane Creative
Editor: Katia Drouillard

Praise for The Road to Purpose

In February 2017, I visited my sister, Carine, at Mission of Grace in Haiti. Upon my arrival, I dealt with mixed emotions because I didn't know how the residents would perceive me. I didn't want to come off being "boujie."

Carine kept telling me not to worry because the people here are so welcoming, loving, and full of spirit. She kept reminding me that I was going to love it here. As my tour began through Mission of Grace, I could immediately feel the love. The children welcomed Carine as if she was a celebrity, yelling "Ms. Carine, Ms. Carine." Carine had been away for two days. When they saw her, they truly had missed her It was present in how they embraced her as we walked and talked. They were constantly hugging her and trying to hold her hand. As we stopped at the teen girls' home, one of the girls told me, "To have a little sister like Ms. Carine is a blessing. We love her and everything she is doing to help us." This very statement warmed my heart. I was only there for about 2 hours, but it was the best 2 hours ever.

My sister is a young, black woman who is giving back to her own culture. She wakes up every day contemplating how she can provide basic needs to Mission of Grace or Haiti in general. Back home in Philadelphia, she hosts donation drives, where people can donate toiletries, money, and/or therapeutic activities. Once the donations are received, it's like the people of Mission of Grace have won the lottery. They are always happy and appreciative for the thought and love they receive from these acts of kindness. I'm proud to call Carine my sister. She is truly a blessing.
Farah Dorlus

Carine's experiences have touched our hearts in more than one way. We were so thrilled when she went back. Her philanthropic nature embodies what it means to care for another human being. Being a Haitian American, naturally we want the best for our country. When Carine visits Haiti, it gives us a sense of pride and hope, hope that with the help of individuals like her, our country will have a better future. Through her stories and accounts, the care and compassion that she has is apparent. Currently, it's hard to pick up and leave the luxuries that we take for granted here in America and move into an environment where life is much different. It takes great courage and resilience to fulfill a journey like this. We hope that many young people will be inspired by Carine's experiences.

Tatiana Drouillard

Here is a book that captures the beauty of what it's like to live fearlessly, yet gracefully in the will of God. Carine's genuine message and heart for our people can be felt with every word and story. This book is more than worth the read. It's a fresh perspective that will allow us to get re-aligned with our purpose while living out our passions.

Meagan Henry
CEO of M Seven Enterprises + Founder of Atlanta For Haiti

Wow! When I think about my overall experience with Carine, I can't help but crack a smile! She is by far one of the most caring, loving, genuine people I know. I don't just call her sis for cool points, I call her sis, because that's what our relationship is built on. Sisterhood! Carine is a supporter, a motivator, not just in words but with her actions! I thank the universe for her daily! The seed that was planted in her is slowly starting to blossom & I'm proud to have watched her journey! Peace, love & blessings to you sis! May you continue to be a blessing & receive every blessing you deserve.

Love always,
Your Sister, Rachel W.

I congratulate you for your hard work and activism in Haiti. Not only have you done marvelous work in Haiti, but also in your hometown of Philadelphia. You are what a Global Citizen encompasses empathy, resilience, and determination to see a better world for those who are less privileged. You have so much more to show and give to this world, continue to follow your dreams and passion.

Jeff Drouillard

Forward

I have had the honor of working with Carine for a little over a year. She came to serve Mission of Grace in January 2017. I remember receiving her application and thinking how amazing it would be for her as a Haitian to come back and serve her people. The founder of Mission of Grace is a beautiful Haitian woman who has made it her life work to give back to her country and encourage other Haitians to do the same. When I received Carine's application and we prayed over it, we were so excited to have her come and serve for 5 months.

When I first saw her, I remember thinking that we needed to put some weight on her because she was so small. But besides her petite frame, she showed me her strength, her beauty, her generosity and her commitment. Carine is someone who would give you the shirt she is wearing without thinking twice, she is someone who never tires, who is very flexible and someone who truly demonstrates loving God and loving others well.

Her main role while working with Mission of Grace was working with our special needs children at the orphanage and school. We really needed someone to spend one on one time with them, and what a blessing it was that Carine spoke creole also. She worked endless hours working with some specific children who we assigned to her. Their growth over the 5 months was amazing both in terms of their physical and emotional development. They grew leaps and bounds.

As Carine shared with me that she was writing this book, it made me think of how different she is today because she stepped out in faith and decided to allow herself to walk into an unknown obedience and an unknown future of serving her country. I hope this book encourages other Haitians to serve their country and discover their purpose in the process.

Carine is precious and called in the name of our Father. She is beautiful and it has been such an honor for me to work so closely with her over this past year and see her growth and her influence. Keep moving Carine, this is just the beginning.

Kim O'Dwyer: Director, Mission of Grace

Dedication

To my beautiful niece, Aniyah, and my talented goddaughter, Saima, this book is dedicated to you. I want you both to always remember that if you work hard you can achieve anything you want.

Love,
Auntie and God mom

Contents

Acknowledgements

Chapter 1: Shit Hole Country	1
Chapter 2: Taking A Leap of Faith	7
Chapter 3: Expect the Unknown	11
Chapter 4: Unknown Village	15
Chapter 5: The White Gates	19
Chapter 6: The Fallen Angel	21
Chapter 7: Bad Habits	25
Chapter 8: Crying Secrets	31
Chapter 9: A Late Start	37
Chapter 10: Divine Love	41
Chapter 11: Dream Team	45
Chapter 12: Failure Equals Success	51
Chapter 13: Philadelphia For Haiti	55
Chapter 14: Just Start	57

Acknowledgements

I would love to express my gratefulness to the many people who have molded and shaped me into the woman I am today, and who have walked alongside me at different moments in my life, and through my adventure in Haiti.

To my amazing family and dear friends, thank you so much. Thank you for supporting my crazy ideas and giving me feedback when I needed it. Thank you for your compassion, support, encouragement and love. Without all of that and more, I know this book would not have been written. Thank you again. You all rock!

Chapter 1

The Shit Hole Country

Haiti (or Ayiti as pronounced in Haitian Creole) has been a country in turmoil for two centuries. This is due to the country's extreme levels of poverty, as well corrupt and unstable governments. Haiti, however, is a secret paradise, full of beautiful sights and wonderful people.
My parents left Haiti in 1984 for the" American Dream." By 1988, my parents had their first child, my older sister Farah. A year later, my parents had to go back to Haiti to receive their green card. Then in 1991, the miracle child was born, me - Carine. My mother suffered major complications during pregnancy, and as a result,

I was born at five months - close to death. My parents call me the miracle child due to everything I had been through. My parents always go back to Haiti to visit family and friends they left behind every year. Both my parents worked two jobs to make ends meet to give my sister and I the best life possible and that's what they did. In June 1996, my parents took their citizenship test, they failed it. Eleven years later, they tried again and passed this time. From that day forward, I knew I had hard working, determined parents who didn't let a failure predict their future.

I first visited Haiti in 2002 when I was a child, but I do not remember much from that trip. The next time I visited Haiti was in July 2014. It was a vacation with family to a part of Haiti called Cazale. It was great to see where my mother and father were from. I really enjoyed myself during that trip. It was great to be with family and basically just being a tourist.

In 2016, at the age of 25 years old, I had plans to complete my undergraduate internship. Haiti was the only country that came to my mind. I'm a firm believer when God places something in your heart it's for you. I just knew it was a must to give back to my Haitian people.

Haiti has had a special place in my heart since birth. Although I was born and raised in the inner city of Philadelphia, Haiti was always a major part of me. For the longest time, it only seemed to be a place that was lost in translation. Growing up, many people I encountered had skewed perspectives of this country. During my younger years, I would not say that I was a Haitian because of all the negative stereotypes it carried.

As a young child, I learned to assimilate into the American culture. I was constantly fighting with my identity because I didn't know much about Haiti's rich culture. As I got older, I realized more that there was something to be said for all the strong Haitian representation in my life. My mother, my relatives were all hard-working, respectable, and culturally oriented people. All it would take to open my eyes to the reality of what Haitian-American meant was to go investigate and research more about Haiti. Haitians have shown a great deal of resilience through history as they have endured so many different adversities. Haiti had to fight several European super powers (France, Spain, Britain) to gain its independence. Imagine a life of fight and resistance, imagine the history being built on the backs of battle. It seemed that this country had always had the ability to bounce back. Half or more of the people can neither read nor write. But wisdom is oral. People hand down their knowledge and express it in proverbs.

Going to Haiti to complete my internship was my only choice. I could have stayed in Philadelphia, but when I was a born, I almost died, every time that plays back in my head, I knew there was a reason why I was brought on this earth. Going to Haiti to serve in my mind was that reason.

Through my journey in Haiti, I learned it wasn't about me, but it was about helping the Haitian people. Once I realize that, I understood waking up every day was a blessing and a gift. It was bigger than me. I understood my WHY, I understood my HOW and I understood my WHAT. Giving back, to me, is part of my heart, not about money or publicity. I knew I had to give back to my parents and my Haitian people and pay it forward. There's a Haitian proverb that I like: "Piti, piti, wazo fe nich li" which means "little by little the bird builds its nest." That's how we can proceed. Little by little, we will start by sharing some conversations about Haiti, which in turn will be conversations about hope, and eventually we can promote change. Little by little.

Chapter 2

Taking a Leap of Faith

Sometimes you don't know why God puts a thought in your head. But I believe the man above already ordained that thought, purpose or vision before we were even in our mother's belly. I say that because I never thought I would have been living in Haiti for five months. A year before my undergraduate internship, I decided I was going to complete it in Haiti. I found Mission of Grace on Instagram. Companies found on social media are sometimes not legit, so I was a bit skeptical. I decided to call a family member who was living in Haiti at the time to ask her about the Mission. She automatically got back to me and said, "Oh, that Mission is Legit." Once I got that news from her, I went to my internship professor, Mr. Strazza, and I told him I found a place for my internship even though I had not actually had any communication with the mission. I asked him if I would be able to go Haiti. He told me, "You can go anywhere in the world."

After getting some clarity from my professor, I messaged the mission on Instagram. It took them about three months for them to get back to me. Finally, a supervisor emailed me the application. After I submitted my application, my college needed information on their end, so I emailed him the questions and I gave them to my professor. Because I didn't attend Penn State's main campus, my professor had to send the questionnaire to them. When main campus got the questionnaire, they gave my professor their response. My professor informed me that main campus denied my request and said the Mission was too church based. My professor told me he was going to fight for me to get back to my home country. He said I had to find a way to prove the mission supported people with disabilities. He said it was the only way the university would condone my internship because my undergraduate degree fell under children and adults with disabilities. That same day, I emailed the supervisor to ask if anyone had a disability at the mission. The supervisor emailed me back with a list of them. I told my professor and he said, "I got you a case and now go make history."

After I received all the information and the cost to complete the internship, I was panicked a bit because I had no idea how I was going to raise $5,000. First, I contacted the global program at Penn State Abington to let them know what I was doing. They told me they were not able to help me raise that type of money, especially for an internship. In August of 2016, I started a t-shirt business called K.I.D.S (which stands for Knowledge, Inspiration, Determination, Success). I wrote a proposal letter to my church, I texted my family and friends, and I made a gofundme account. By the end of December, I was able to raise the $5,000 to go to Haiti.

I want to tell you all reading this book: whatever you want to do never give up. With patience and persistence, it can get done. I'm a firm believer of that because it happened to me.

As many times as I wanted to find another place than Haiti because things weren't happening on my time, I just had to trust God and let him figure it all out. I did that and I got the blueprint.

Chapter 3

Expect the Unknown

Arriving to Haiti was one of the scariest things. There were so many people at the airport just hanging around and workers wanting to help. When I got my suitcases from baggage claim, there were two workers wanting to help me. I told them in creole: "mwen pa bezwen okenn èd" which means "I don't need any help." I walked away, struggling with two over 50lbs suitcases. I went outside to look for the driver who was supposed to be wearing an Ocean View shirt and holding a sign. No one was there. I became nervous, thinking "what did I get myself into." I was crying and I was scared. I calmed myself down remembering I was home. If push came to shove, I had family I could reach out to. After a few minutes, I decided to called Ms. Kim from my Haiti phone because I didn't know what to do. I told her I didn't see anyone with an Ocean View shirt or sign. She said the driver was on his way. He was late because my flight had been delayed. Although I was annoyed and disturbed, I managed to stay calm and collected until the driver finally arrived around 2:00 p.m.

The driver gave my luggage to another driver and walked me to the car. The driver pus all my stuff in and told me to get in the car, then locked all doors and stood outside. I was anxious and wondered what was going on. Ms. Kim called and asked if Jerome was with me. I told her no, it was some other guy. I was so scared for my life; I did not know what was going on. Ms. Kim reassured me and told me the driver was going to take me to Ocean View resort before going to the mission. I was really annoyed because I was hungry, thirsty and had a headache. The driver put his seatbelt on, and I put mine on too. I put my head down and prayed. As we drove, I saw clusters of tents, piles of trash and chaos everywhere. The humid air was heavy on my skin, and I smelled sewage through the open windows. I'd already been to Haiti twice, but this time things seemed worse than on my previous visits. The sweat began to bead down my face as we dodged motorcycles, trucks, cars, and children. The ride was silent, except for the thousands of people we passed by who were selling things on the side of the road. My phone rang and Ms. Kim said I had an hour until I arrived. She asked me what I wanted for dinner. I told her Haitian food was fine. She said okay.

One hour later we finally arrived at the resort. I got out of the van and told the driver Jerome to hand me my luggage. I looked at the driver timidly saying "mesi" which is thank you. Waiting to welcome me was Adriane, Ms. Kim's assistant. Ocean View was one beautiful and peaceful. The property was surrounded by palm trees. The people were hospitable. I would get to enjoy many sunrises and sunsets, as well as blue ocean water during my stay. It was the best escape anyone could have.

Chapter 4

An unknown Village

How would you feel if you live somewhere and nobody knew you or that town existed? Well, that is the case for the people of Carries, Haiti. Carries is located 1 hour north of the International Airport in Port-Au-Prince. In 2009, a mudslide and heavy rain destroyed the village of Carries. About 800 people were affected, injured, or died as a result. A year later in 2010, an earthquake struck the entire country of Haiti, killing about 230,000 people. The country is still struggling from the aftermath of this tragedy. In 2015, Carries had another mudslide which destroyed over forty homes in the mountain. Many families lost their homes, were injured, or died. The founder of Mission of Grace, alongside a few other benefactors, continue to work together to rebuild those houses.

When I decided to go on this trip to complete my internship for my undergrad, there were so many friends and family members telling me not to go because they hadn't heard of the village. Comments such as "Haiti is not safe, they will kill you, isn't it poor there? don't they have AIDS?, etc." flooded my messages. I didn't let their negativity discourage me. They couldn't see how I was pursuing my purpose (even though I didn't know it yet). Instead they projected their fears on me and wanted to make me believe that just because they couldn't, I too couldn't. Never give Naysayers a chance.

None of the negative comments I heard about Carries were true. 'Carries is divided by one major street with a beautiful beach front on one side and the village on the other side. When you leave the gates of Ocean View and cross to the village, it's totally a different world. To me, it was the best of two worlds. In the village, there was dusty rocky roads, goats, chickens, and pigs just walking around. There was trash everywhere. There were no locks, no protection, no doors on the houses, just sheets covering the entrance. Children lingered through the village all day long. For a month straight, each time I left the village, I cried in my room. I wanted to pack up my belongings and leave. I just couldn't understand why Haiti was like that. When my family and friends called me, I lied and said everything okay.

Chapter 5

The White Gates

Mission of Grace has two orphanages. One for babies through five years old; the other for kids six through 16. The first day I walked into the orphanage all of the children shouted "gade ti fi blan," which means "look at the white girl." They ran up to me to give me hugs and pull on my long braids. Adriane, Ms. Kim's assistant, asked if I could help her do an activity with the children. She put my creole on the spot by asking me to translate for her. I handled it well.

After a couple of weeks, I finally got to know all of the children. During the afternoons, every day for 2 hours, I worked with the little children, coloring and working on number recognition with them. It was so hard giving all of the children my attention. There were 70 kids, all calling Ms. Carine at one point or another.

One day, I was playing on the swing with a couple of children. As I was pushing one of the toddlers, I stopped and looked around. A thought came to my mind and it was "you have to be voice for them." From that day forward, I knew my life changed, and Carries Haiti had a place in my heart.

Chapter 6

The Fallen Angel

Dr. Seuss wrote in his book <u>Happy Birthday to You</u>, "Today you are You, that is truer than true. There is no one alive who is Youer than You." Every essence of our being, from our personalities to our DNA is different from everyone else in this world. Lamentably, the incapacitated are for the most part avoided in Haiti. There is long-standing apprehension among the general population, particularly those in the mountains, that on the off chance that somebody experiences either a physical or mental handicap, that he or she is possessed by the devil.

There is noticeable discrimination against people with disabilities, which is deeply ingrained within Haitian culture. Many people feel that a disabled child will bring harm to other children and parents often abandon such children. In Haiti, one in ten people are disabled and those with special needs are often treated badly. Discrimination against disabled children is common, with many children with physical or mental disabilities permanently left at home and denied the right to become a part of everyday life. Due to a severe lack of education in the area of disabilities, many families simply don't know what's wrong with their children or how to care for them, sadly resulting in many being abandoned at an early age.

There was a little boy named Jonas with soft hair, long eyelashes, and a welcoming smile but he suffered from Cerebral Palsy. When I was given my assignment to do physical therapy with someone who had a disability, I was anxious because I never worked with someone who had a severe disability. With the limited internet access, I googled what type of daily exercises to do with him.

On January 17, 2017, an older woman came to serve at the mission for two days. She was a therapist. When she found out that I would be working with Jonas, she asked if she would be able to join me. We walked over to the children orphanage. She asked me to translate the exercises for the nannies. She recommended that they have Jonas do them daily. When we were in the room, we took him out of his crib and laid him down on his mat. She looked over to me and said he had Spastic Cerebral Palsy. She explained that it was a developmental disorder caused by damage to the brain before birth, during delivery, or within the first few years of life. Imagine being so stiff and not being able to move at all, well that was the case for little Jonas. Sometimes, while doing range of motion exercises with Jonas and teaching the nannies also, some of the nannies in the room would call him 'Cocobe,' the Creole word for a person with disabilities. It roughly translates as 'worthless' or 'disgraceful. I used to get so upset I cried. But then I had to realize some of the nannies lacked education or just didn't. Proverbs 31:8 says "Speak up for those who cannot speak for themselves." From that day on, I prayed and asked God to help be a voice for the special needs children. Every day for 4 ½ months straight, Monday through Friday, I did range of motion exercises with Jonas and thought the nannies as well. I saw so much progress in him. At one point in time, he could not move his neck from left to right it was so stiff. But with my consistent help, he was able to move his neck left to right. Jonas thought me so much patience. Because of him, I have a love for special needs children.

Unfortunately, Jonas passed away February 6,2018 at the age of five. He is not suffering or in pain anymore.

Chapter 7

Bad Habits

Chantale is beautiful, 15-year old young lady who a missionary asked me to help counsel. The missionary came to me one afternoon in March asking if I could help her with a situation. The missionary informed me that at sunset, Chantale went outside and ate rocks. The next day, I walked over to the orphanage in the hot 90-degree sun, up the rocky mountain, sweat dripping down my face. When I got to the orphanage, the children were singing in Creole "Here is Ms. Carine." I walked over to Chantale room and asked if I could talk to her. She said okay, looking very shy. I told her the missionary was very worried about her. I told her she had nothing to worry about if it was true. Then, I asked her if she ate rocks. She said, "Wi Ms. Carine" meaning, "Yes, Ms. Carine." I asked her why. She told me when she was little she used to be so hungry and there was nothing for me to eat, so she ate rocks to rocks to fill her up. She said she wanted to stop but she didn't know how to. I looked at her and tears started to fall down my face, but I told her I would do my best to help her, but she had to want to help herself with this addiction.

After writing my notes, I went straight to texting my internship Professor telling him about this young lady's behavior. I just knew I had to do something to help her. He texted me back with information saying she had a disorder called Pica. While doing my research with the limited internet access I had, I discovered that Pica was an eating disorder typically defined as the persistent ingestion of nonnutritive substances for at least 1 month at an age for which this behavior is developmentally inappropriate. It may be benign or may have life-threatening consequences.

When I was done researching, I came up with the following behavior strategy treatment plan. First, I decided to interview her to understand when she exhibited the behavior. Generally, it sounded like it was more of an emotional need. The interview revealed the following: She ate rock every day when she was hungry. She didn't know if she was substituting the rocks for something else. She shared whenever the sun came down, she reached for the rocks. Eating them was so painful that she would sometimes vomit. She said it hurt her throat when she swallowed them. She also would have stomach pains for a week.

While continuing my research, I had to take it another step further by doing a paradoxical intervention. Paradoxical interventions are psychotherapeutic tactics that seem to contradict the goals they are designed to achieve. For example, a therapist may prescribe that clients deliberately have an unwanted symptom or restrain them from changing. This intervention is something that is not popular anymore, but it was something that I thought would be very effective to use in this situation. For example: I would tell Chantale to suck on as many rocks as she wanted in the daytime, but only eat a few rocks at dinner time for dessert. If she wanted to suck on rocks at night, we could talk about it but only if she did not swallow at night. PS sucking on rocks is seen as nutritious. I would use different paradoxical strategies to decrease control and then show her how she actually had control over the behavior because she was able to change. I knew this would be fun in a therapeutic way.

I gave Chantale a notebook. She looked at me like I was crazy. I told her this activity would be fun. I told her when she started to feel like she was about to go outside when the sun went down, she had to pick up this notebook and write or draw whatever that came to her mind. A month later, she came and handed me this book filled with 20 pages of things she just wrote to me. I didn't expect her to have so much writing. She shared that she had not eaten rocks in a while and credited me for helping her. I told Chantale it was not about me, but about her. I helped but she put in the effort for a whole month and that made me so proud of her.

If you know anyone who has a behavior such as the one Chantale had or whatever the case is and you feel it inside of you that you can do something to help that person, please do. You never know just being by that person's side can help stop addiction. I never thought that I would help a young lady like her while being in Haiti, but with persistence and presence, I showed her a sense of love and I cared about her well-being.

Chapter 8

Crying Secrets

During my time in Haiti, I kept asking God "why am I here? What do you want to do or bring to the mission?" One day while watching the sunset go down sitting on the Gazebo, listening to the waves go back and forth, I heard a voice say, "get to know each the 18 teen girls." Every day from that moment, I ate lunch with the teen girls. Their nannie Madame Tamara cooked me some amazing food. At first, the girls did not engage with me. I would say something in Creole, "Koman ou ye," which means "How are you?" but wouldn't get a response. I was determined to find a way to get these girls to talk to me. Every day for two hours, I made it my business to go to their house and just sit there regardless if they talked to me or not. Eventually, they started to be more open. These teen girls had been through so much it broke my heart. Some of the things they had been through like abuse, neglect, rape by family and friends were unfathomable. They had so much bottled in and they were never able to share any of it because they never had anyone to talk to until I came. Together we built trust.

While there, this lady named Keisha came to serve at the mission. One day after breakfast, I spoke briefly with her about how we can help the girls. We both came up with the idea of doing visions boards. The next day we decided to do the activity with them. Keisha explained what a vision was, what a vision board was, and what a vision board did. I translated for her in Creole. That day, we had magazines, posters, scissors, glue and the girls got to work. To see how the girls grasped the concept was truly amazing. Each of them had real life goals for their future. When we were done, we asked for at least five of them to explain their vision to us. One of the girl's vision was to adore God for the rest of her life, get married and have children. She wanted to have a house that had a library in it for her children. Most of all, she wanted to become a counselor to help children and adults who were in her shoes to help them leave their past alone and become better versions of themselves.

I realized they were the most natural, beautiful, Haitian young girls I had ever met. Everything about them was natural. They had no name brand clothing, no electronics, nothing. I poured into them and they poured into me. Some days, they were upset with me and didn't even want to talk. Some days were filled with laughter and smiles. They gave me compliments every day that warmed my heart. On April 19, 2017 I texted Ms. Kim and asked if I could take the girls on a trip to Port au Prince, the capital of Haiti. She said yes. With money I had left over, The missionary and I decided to take the girls to eat pizza at a restaurant called Munchies. The driver and I went to the orphanage to pick them up. When they got in the van they put on their best clothes and were just smiling. Some of the girls were so happy because it was their first time leaving the village of Carries and getting into a vehicle. I just couldn't believe it. I had so many thoughts running through my head during that trip. We had to stop by two different villages because some of the girls were getting car sick and were vomiting. Three of the girls were so sick they had to keep their heads out the window to get air. I had never seen anything like it before. The driver looked at me and asked if I wanted to return to Carries. I asked the girls and they said no, they had never been anywhere, and they wanted to go. I tapped the driver's shoulder and said to continue driving. When we finally got to the restaurant about 2 hours later, it was time to order the pizza. I told the girls to look at the menu and pick two kinds they would like. They looked at me and said "Ms. Carine, this is the first time we are eating pizza and we don't know what's good; how about you order for us." When the waiter came over, I ordered cheese and pepperoni - the basic. When the pizza arrived, the girls chose what they wanted. The girls were cutting the pizza with the knife and folks, I busted out laughing, "girls what are you doing, in the United States we pick of the pizza with our hands and eat it. They looked at me like I was crazy. I told them to try it. It was the funniest thing to watch them eat pizza. That trip was one for the best for me. I was glad I was able to provide this experience that would mean so much to them.

The day before I left May 1, 2017, I made bags of clothes for each of the girls. I gave each of them 3 outfits: tops and bottoms, and jewelry. I folded them nicely and put in plastic bags and wrote their names on it. I packed the eighteen bags and put them in the suitcase and asked Ms. Kim to take me to the orphanage. When I got to the girls' house, they were all sitting on the porch. I thanked each girl for healing me. I had always had a relationship with God but being here with them made my faith stronger than ever before. I took a deep breath and I started to talk to each girl, telling them to always keep God first in whatever, whenever, and wherever they are going. I told them to continue and push through school and most of all to follow their dreams because the little children are looking up to them, they were the leaders of this mission so be the change. As I was opening the suitcase, tears started to fall down my face before I handed each girl her bag. I poured into them affirmation, talents and gifts that I observed from them day one I led eyes on them. As I watched the girls cry as I gave them their gift, I thought to myself "Carine you have now built a sisterhood." Moments of silence and crying, out of nowhere one of the girls named Nadia started to worship unexpectedly and told all the girls to circle around me singing in Creole *"Mwen gen yon papa, Ki relem pam, Li pap Janm Kite mwen Nenpot kote m ale, Li konnen non m. Li konnen tout panse, Li we chak fwa m kriye, E li tande le m rele."*

In English Translation it says, *"I* have a good father, who calls me his, he won't never leave me wherever I go, he knows my every thought, he sees every time I cry, he hears me when I yell." After that Nadia told each girl to say something over me since I would be returning home and graduating May 5, 2017. Tears were falling down my eyes; I was just lost for words. Ms. Kim looked at me as we are leaving and she said "Carine, that was the most powerful thing the girls had ever done, that was beautiful".

As I left those whites gates, I realized each one of those girls had become my little sisters. They were not sisters by blood, but my sisters by heart. They taught me HUMILITY and GRATITUDE in the most GRACIOUS WAY.

Chapter 9

A Late Start

How would you feel if someone kept telling you are worthless, you will never be nothing since you were born? How would you feel if you were 17 and could not read or write? That was the case for beautiful Beatrice. Beatrice used to live next door at Children of Grace. She was beaten every day of her life, which resulted in hearing loss. Just last year, the founder of the mission heard the news and decided to bring her into the teen girls' home. In Haiti, school is not free so if your parents do not have a job, you are not able to go to school. All of her seventeen years of living she had not attended school until 2016. She was put in the first grade, not knowing how to read and write.

I met Beatrice the first week of February at the Grace Community School. I became her one to one in the classroom. At times, it was just so hard for me to work with her due to the classroom being so loud. At times, the teacher wouldn't even recognize her while I was there. I decided to ask the principal if I could use his office three times a week. The principal said yes. Once I got that answer, I knew it was on from there. I had no idea how I was going to do it, then I realized I had to start from scratch with her. The resources I used were flashcards with basic colors and a kindergarten's small chalkboard. She looked at me like I was crazy. There were days when it was so hot in the office, both of us were sweating and crying. It was hard. I remember I wanted to just give up on her, but I didn't. I knew the outcome would be great. For the first couple of weeks, she couldn't do it. "I can't do it," was her refrain. I got tired of hearing her speaking so negatively of herself, so every day before we started, I had her repeat the positive affirmation "I can do it." I worked with her from 10 am to 2 pm every day. It was not easy all.

There were days the girls she lived with would make fun of her and said unkind words to her to the point she would cry. I told them she was just like them. Regardless of her disability, we needed to work together to help her. When they realized how hard I worked with her, they noticed she was able to do it. By the end of March, I felt so accomplished because she was able to comprehend color recognition, write in cursive, write her numbers and so much more. I couldn't believe I made an impact in her life. One day, while I was walking down the mountain from church, an old lady tapped my shoulder and said to me, "I hear you are the one working with my granddaughter and she is improving, I just want to tell you Thank You So Much." The day I left, she was one of the girls who took it hard, literally. She never had someone like me believe in her, and for that I never gave up on her, not one bit.

Even though Beatrice had a late start to her schooling, she was still able to learn and grasp information she never thought she could do. I'm a firm believer that it's never too late to start or do anything in life. People always told me I must have my life figured out in a certain way, but that is not the case at all. Sometimes, life hits us in a way we least expect it. "For what it's worth: it's never too late or, in my case, too early to be whoever you want to be. There's no time limit, stop whenever you want. You can change or stay the same, there are no rules to this thing. We can make the best or the worst of it. I hope you make the best of it. And I hope you see things that startle you. I hope you feel things you never felt before. I hope you meet people with a different point of view. I hope you live a life you're proud of. If you find that you're not, I hope you have the strength to start all over again." -F. Scott Fitzgerald

Chapter 10

Divine Love

On February 26, 2016, a 41-year old woman came to the clinic saying she wanted to abandon her baby. She had visited the clinic 3-4 times before making similar claims without following through. That afternoon, she was checked by the nursers. After getting her vitals checked, she was asked to stay in line. When it was time to see the doctor, she sat the baby boy on the exam table. Someone called Ms. Lynn to let her know this lady wanted to abandon her baby. With no answer, the nursers left a message on her phone. A few minutes later, the lady ran off and left the little baby boy on the exam table. He had no health chart with his name or age. Two months passed and this little boy started to have lung complications. He developed pneumonia and almost passed away. For about 6 months, due to lack of education and health care resources, all he did was lay in his crib. Due to that he became developmentally delayed in his fine and gross motor skills.

This little boy's name was Ermias. I met him on January 18, 2017 and when I first laid eyes on him all I could do was cry and hold him close to my heart. From that moment, I knew God had given me a son. Hearing his story, I could not believe it. I had a feeling in my heart that he needed to be loved by me.

When I was started to work with him helping him crawl, he cried every day. The first day he crawled for me, I was so happy, and he gave me a smirk smile, like "Carine I don't want to do this. can't you see it." But I knew he was a fighter and I knew he would crawl.

As time progressed, I started to feel like I had to start mothering him. "To mother" means to teach, and teaching is my purpose. Teaching him to crawl and doing range of motions activities with him taught me that he was able to do anything. There were days when as I was leaving the orphanage to return to Ocean View, he would cry after me because he knew and felt my intentions were pure. The day before I left, I prayed for him and I told him thank you for coming into my life. I told him I would see him again. We prayed, I kissed and hugged him, then sat him down on the orphanage floor. Ermias made my stay in Haiti easier. I wasn't his birth mother, but I knew I had become his adopted mom from a far.

Chapter 11

Dream Team

I believe a dream team is a group of people who are willing to work together to get the job done. While in Haiti, there were several people who helped my transition and journey become smoother. There was a pastor who came from Tennessee named Richard. He talked to us all about the definition of a dream team and about three important Cs that we needed to keep with us. The 3 Cs are Character, Competence and Chemistry. He said to remember those three things whenever we interacted with each other. When he said that to me, it really made sense because each of one of us were placed at Mission of Grace during that time for a specific reason.

The people that follow made up my Dream Team:
1. Linotte Joseph: Ms.Lynn is the founder of Mission of Grace. She was born and raised in Haiti. She was such an important factor to me during my time in Haiti. When she first met me, she said to me: "Thank you so much for coming to serve at Mission of Grace. You are the first American Haitian in college to complete your internship in Haiti, that speaks volume." She became my momma for this journey.
2. Kim O'Dwyer: Kim is the director of Mission of Grace. She was very reserved. She left her Canadian home to come serve the Haitian people. She could have been anywhere in the world but she chose Haiti. She taught me to become strong, have faith in everything I do, and most of all to FINISH STRONG. One bible scripture that reminds me of her is Philippians 2:3 which says "Do nothing out of selfish ambition or vain conceit. Rather, in humility value others above yourselves." This scripture is so true about how she valued others above herself.

3. Adriane: She served as an assistant to Miss Kim and helped to lead and coordinate with our short-term teams on the ground. One thing I learned from her is to never give up. Although she didn't know how to speak Creole, she did not give up for anything. She was one of most determined people I came across.
4. Krista: She was my roommate for 2 months. She had such a free spirit and at the age of 19 moved to live in Haiti. She taught me it was okay not to have it all figured out.
5. Meagan: A beautiful woman from Atlanta GA. She was my roommate for 2 weeks and one night she told me: "I think you should write a book about your experience." Although she didn't know me from a can of paint, she said before she left Haiti, she would create a website for me to promote my work in Haiti. And she did "philly4haiti.com." I was literally speechless. I learned it was important to "strike while it's hot." She taught me to fear nothing, and just live life to the fullest potential.

6. Sandra: She was the sweetest, most soft-spoken person I ever met. She was from Canada. She taught English at the Grace School and to the community. She was a fighter and always got the job done, no matter what. It was a great lesson for me.
7. Howard: This man had the most amazing testimony. He has had some trials and tribulations, but God turned his life around and now he was living and serving in Haiti. He started a baseball team for the boys in the orphanage. Every Wednesday, the children come to Ocean View Resort and practice on the tennis court with the little that they had. Howard got all the construction done for Mission of Grace.
8. Madame' Luc: During my time in Haiti, I had the opportunity to meet Ms. Lynn's mother. Her soul was so pure, one could feel it inside. When she first met me, she said "You remind me of Ms. Lynn when she your age, keep being a leader and everything will pay off Carine. You have leadership skills inside of you already."

The most important thing I learned from each one of these different individuals is that people who you do not know are going to root for you.

And sometimes, it's not intentional, it's because these people want to see you win. They supported and uplifted me throughout my journey, and for that, I am grateful.

Chapter 12

Failure equals Success

Growing up, I believed failure was the end of world. Either one failed or succeeded. But as I got older, I started to realize that failure could equal success. Back in 2015, I was attending Penn State Berks Campus majoring in Early Childhood Education. I was taking an intro to special needs class. The whole semester I was passing the class with a high B. A week before finals week, I had a meeting with the professor about my final paper and she told me bluntly that I wasn't fit to be a teacher. When she said that, I looked at her and asked her how would she know I wasn't fit to be teacher? I left the meeting without talking to her. When I received my final grade for the class, it was an F. I could not believe. I wrote a letter to the Dean of Students explaining how I felt about the comment and the failing grade. They investigated, but the outcome didn't change. I still had an F and had to change my major. I transferred back to Penn State Abington. While transferring to Penn State Abington I changed my major to Rehabilitation and Human Services. I found myself really enjoying the major until something happened my senior year that almost made me unable to complete my internship in Haiti. I was taking an online Abnormal Psychology class at another Penn State Campus. Maybe two weeks before the class ended, the professor emailed me and another student accusing us of plagiarism. I emailed the professor explaining that I didn't know what he was referring to. He stated that my work and the work of another student were very similar, and we were both in the same major. Although we were on different campuses, the professor decided to fail both of us for the class. This grade was going to jeopardize my internship in Haiti, but professor Strazza said he would help me in any way he could. Unfortunately, the grade stood, and I had to retake Abnormal Psychology at a different college while in Haiti.

It was a struggle to get things done with that class due to the lack of consistent internet access, but I did. It was April 6, 2017, I decided that morning I was going to handle graduation stuff and get my transcript sent over from one school to another. Grades didn't go in for the online Abnormal Psychology class until May 1, 2017, but Penn State needed all graduating senior grades by April 28. I emailed Penn State letting them know my issue; they emailed me back saying they would give me extension until May 5, 2017. Then I called Montgomery community college explaining my situation. The transcript people on the phone told me to email my advisor, which I did. The advisor told me to email my professor for the class. I did that. Less than an hour later, the Montgomery professor told me she would grant me permission to send all my work to her by that Friday and she would put my grade in early for me. I passed the class with an A+ and was able to send my transcript and be set for graduation

What I learned from each of those situations is that you must fail in order to succeed. I didn't let that professor's comment deter my life. When you google the word failure, the definition that comes up is lack of success, but I believe that is not true. I believe failure is what gets you through those difficult times and pushes you harder to succeed. There's a guy I met back in 2015 at a Philadelphia Conference. His name was Inky Johnson. He became one of my favorite motivational speakers. I still follow him on Instagram and everyday he puts something on his page that's inspiring. The most important thing I got from him was this quote, "Failure is not the opposite of success…. It's a part of it!" To be honest, I thank both of those situations for happening because who's to say I'd be the woman I am now. Always remember failure is temporary., It's what you learn after failing that matters the most.

Chapter 13

Philadelphia For Haiti

I knew when I had finished my internship in Carries, that I would have to come back to continue fulfilling my purpose. I can honestly say Philly4Haiti started when I had the vision to go to Haiti and serve. However, it didn't come into fruition until February 2018. Philly4Haiti serves as a Philadelphia based conduit for inventive, cultural, spiritual, and empowering Haiti outreach initiatives. Haiti is one of the least literate countries in the world. The unemployment and poverty rates are staggering. Our mission is to help take care of our Haitian people in any way possible.

My goal is to curate experiences and give people around the world a taste of the beauty of Haiti while giving back. We have done back to school drives, teen girls and boys outreach events, etc. So far, I have brought numerous groups of people to Haiti and they shared testimonies with me that made me cry every time I read them.

Serving others prepares you to lead others. There's nothing like walking in your purpose and having people follow you. It has been such a humbling feeling to connect people in the service of the Haitian people.

Chapter 14

Just Start

I don't chase dreams anymore. Rather, I chase my purpose because that is why I was put on this earth and it will never change. I read a book called <u>The Purpose Driven Life</u> by Rick Warren. In one chapter, he states "the purpose of life is far greater than your own personal fulfilment, your peace of mind, or even your happiness. It's far greater than your family, your career, or even your wildest dreams and ambitions. If you want to know why you were placed on this planet, you must begin with God. You were born by his purpose and for his purpose." When I think of the word "purpose," I define it as what sets the soul on fire. Once you realize what sets your soul on fire, you will know what your purpose is.

I'm here to tell you whatever it is that you want to do in life, just do it. Don't listen to anyone who haven't been in your shoes. A friend of mine told me "Stop Seeking advice from people who are content with being robots and living safe." - Neesh M. What I took from that is your vision is your vision only. I'm the type of person I walk to my own beat of the drum. Whatever it is that I want to do I'm going to do. I don't need anyone's approval. I realize I can't worry about people's opinions because they don't really understand me anyway. Love people for who they are and stop sharing your ideas with people who don't see your vision. Believe in yourself and the rest is invincible.

I read a book by a man called Marcus Y. Rosier called <u>Win the Day</u>. It's such a great book. In it, the author breaks down a scenario that happens to be true and everyone should use. "Win the Day is a time management life practice in which you convert time into money. The concept is to make every hour of the day worth $100. The entire day is worth $2,400. The goal is to pay the areas of your life that are most important a minimum of $240 (2 hours and 40 minutes) each day. Anything less than that, and you have lost the day." We all have the same number of hours in the day, and it doesn't hurt to spend any time on your purpose. Write down your goals. Once you write them down, they are more likely to come to fruition. Work hard each day, regardless of how lonely the process may be, it's okay. Just don't quit when it gets hard. Use that as motivation to push harder, and most of all, stay humble through the process, it will all pay off in the long run. Remember it doesn't have to be perfect; if you've started, you've won.

God gave me strength, power, favor, and abundance to keep on going through the trials and tribulations of my time in Haiti. I did not give up! I met so many wonderful people from all different parts of the world! I was showered with kindness throughout the village of Carries! Regardless of the people's circumstances, they were always smiling and embracing! They showed me how to find joy in the simple things. Despite their dire conditions, they always found joy! This experience has been more than completing a requirement for my undergraduate degree, God changed my path. He needed me in Carries to do physical therapy at the elderly home and with Jonas, to be a one-to-one tutor to

Beatrice at the school to help her learn to write and recognize colors and numbers, to be a translator at times (which was not easy), to give my Ermias love each and every day at the orphanage, to pour into the hearts of the teen girls and to expand their horizons.

What I learned through my journey is that you must appreciate where you are in your process, even if it's not where you want to be. Every season serves a purpose. God has a plan for you. He can use you regardless of how old or young you are. God gives everyone a gift. Take the time to figure out yours. It will not happen overnight, but once you know, no one can tell you differently. Know that God has a plan for you and his way is the best way. When you take the high road, God has your back. Know that some amazing things are about to happen in your life. But it starts with you believing in yourself first. Through the process of discovering my purpose, I had to trust God, pray, be obedient, fast, discipline myself, serve others. It made me become the best version of myself. I have been filled with overflowing joy! My internship in Haiti changed my life. I found my purpose.

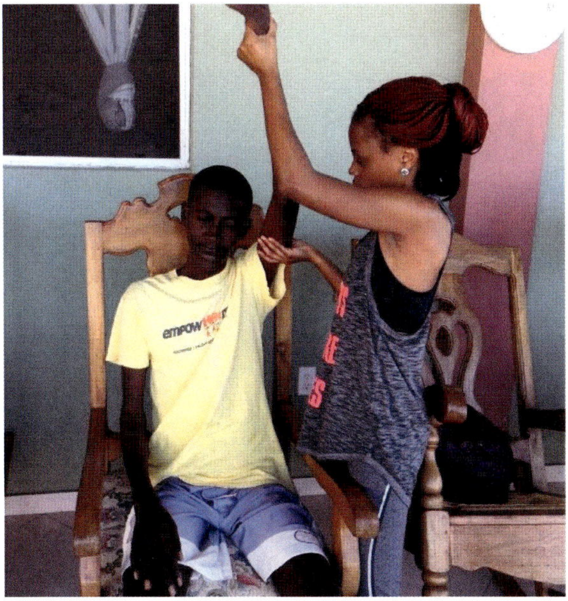

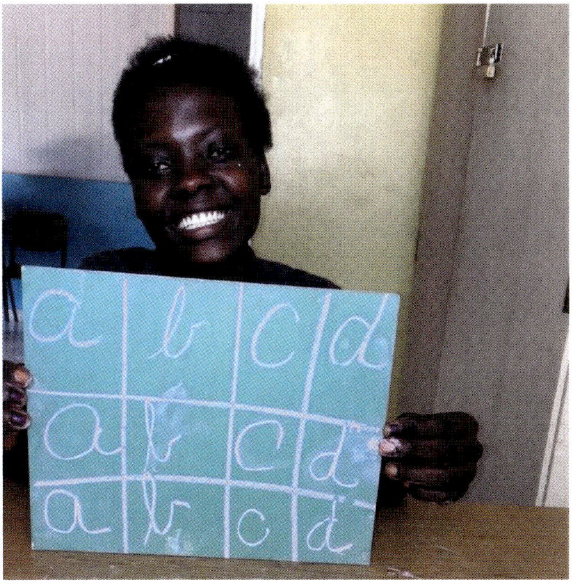
a b c d
a b c d
a b c d

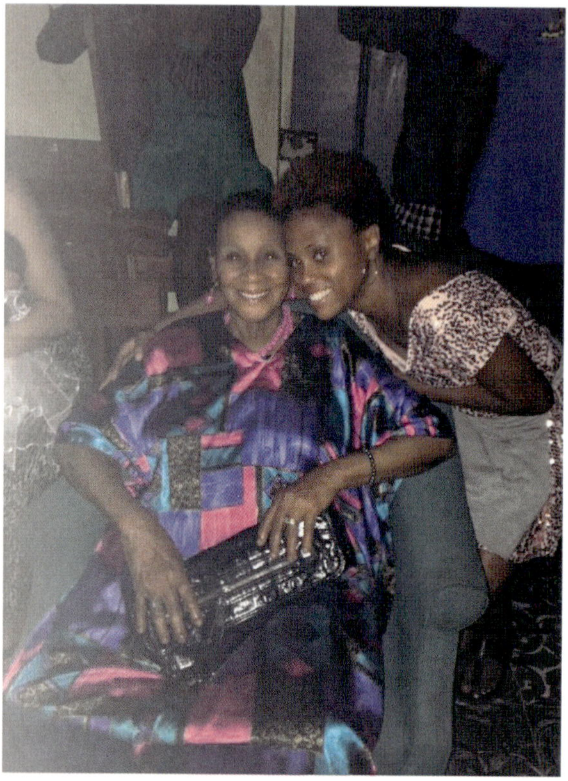

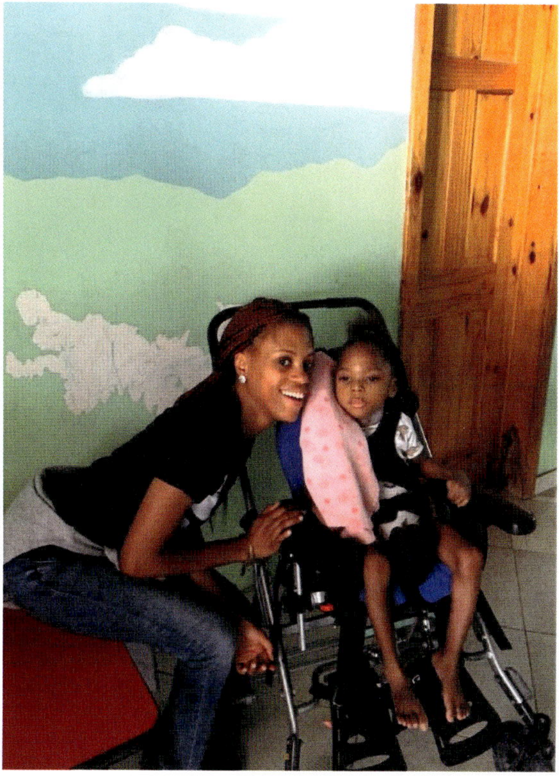

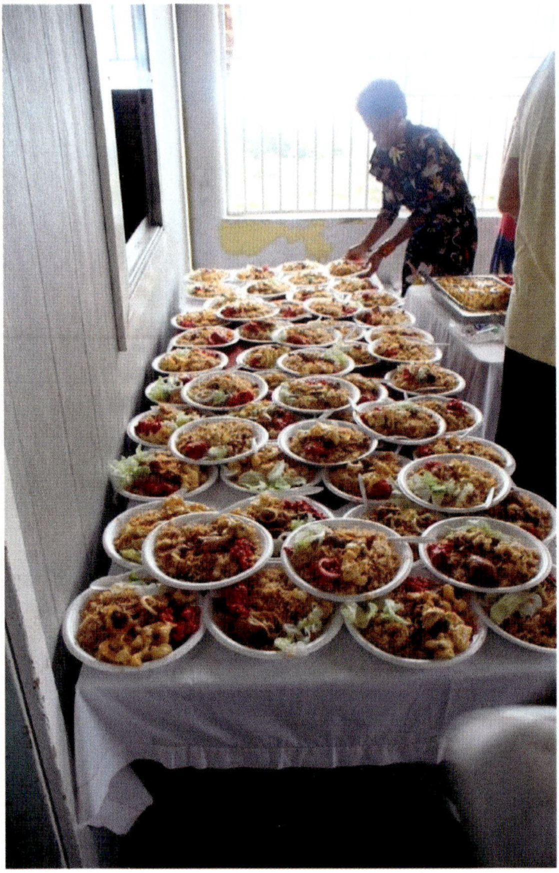

The Road to Purpose

Green
verde
Square
el cuadrado
Black
Diamond
Triangle
Oval
Oval
Square
el cuadrado

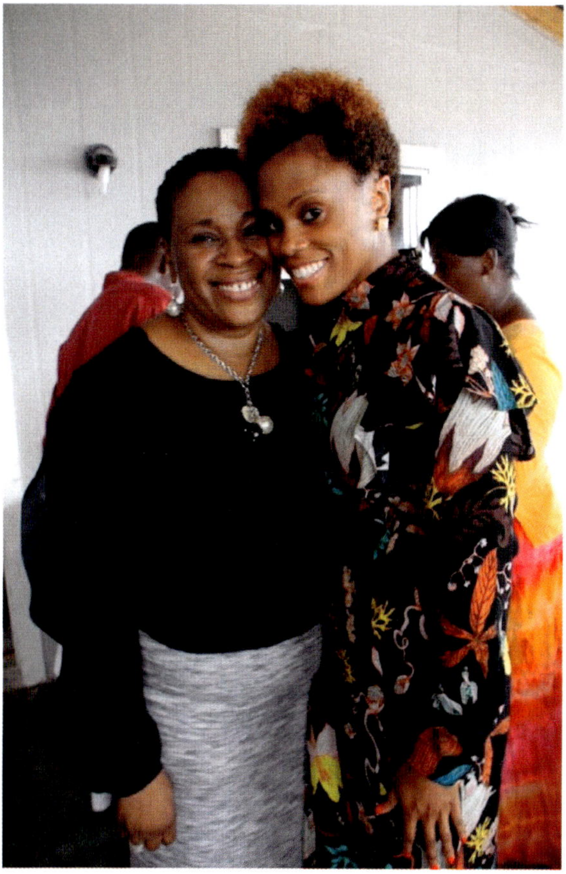

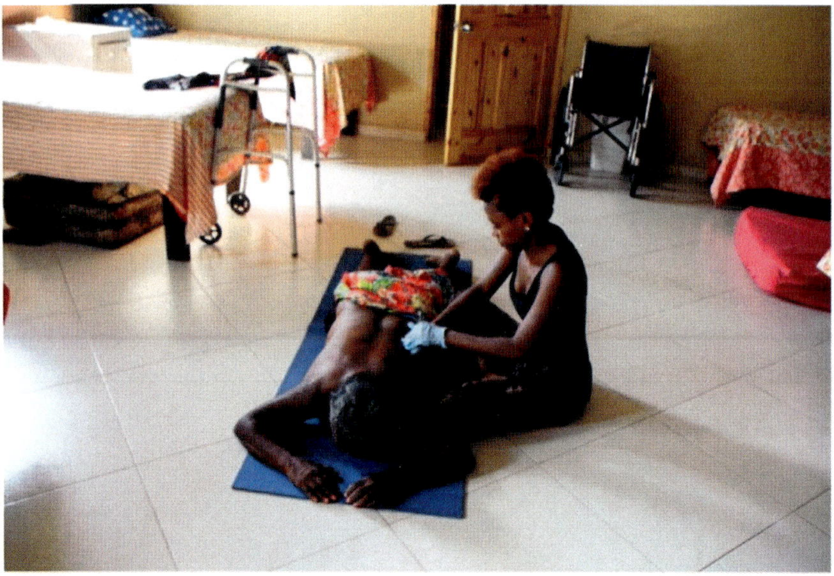

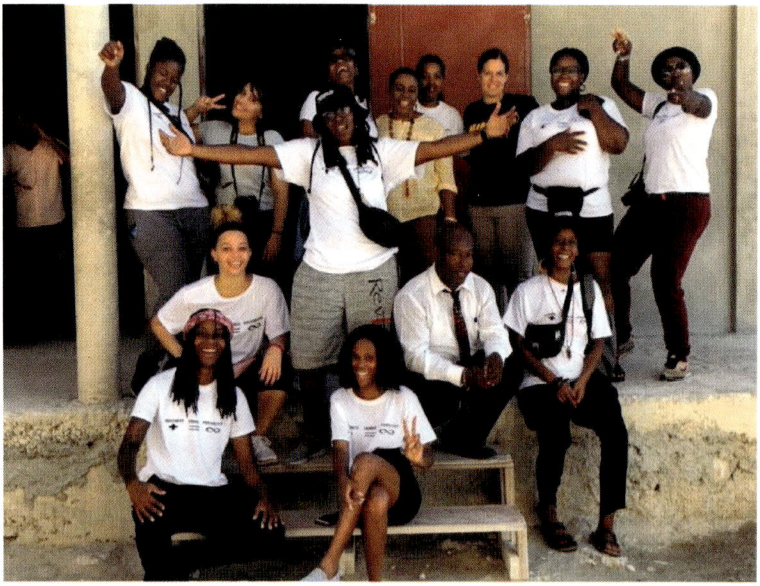

The Road to Purpose

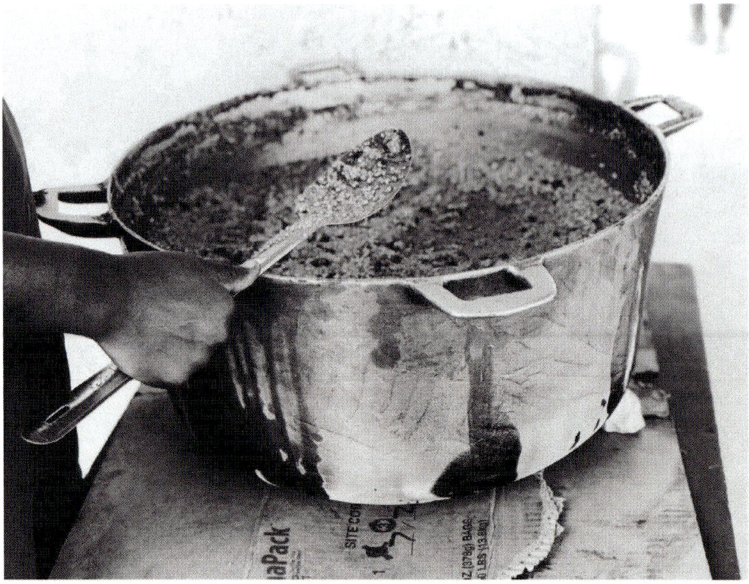

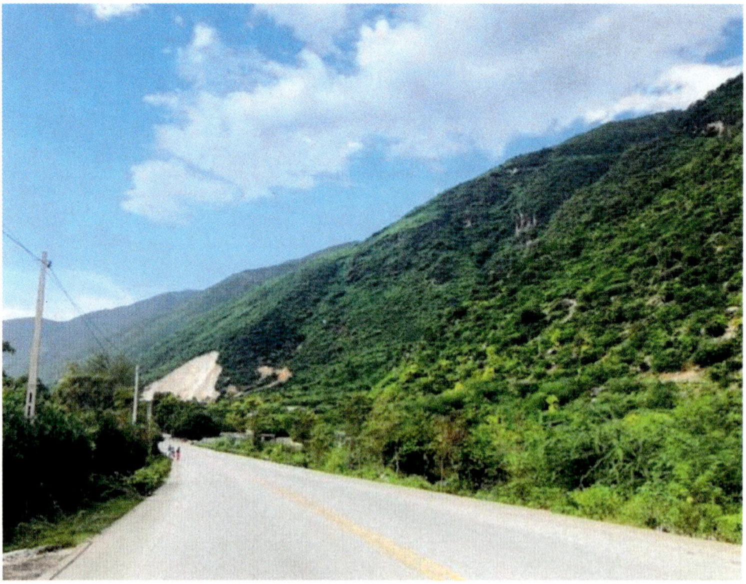

The Road to Purpose

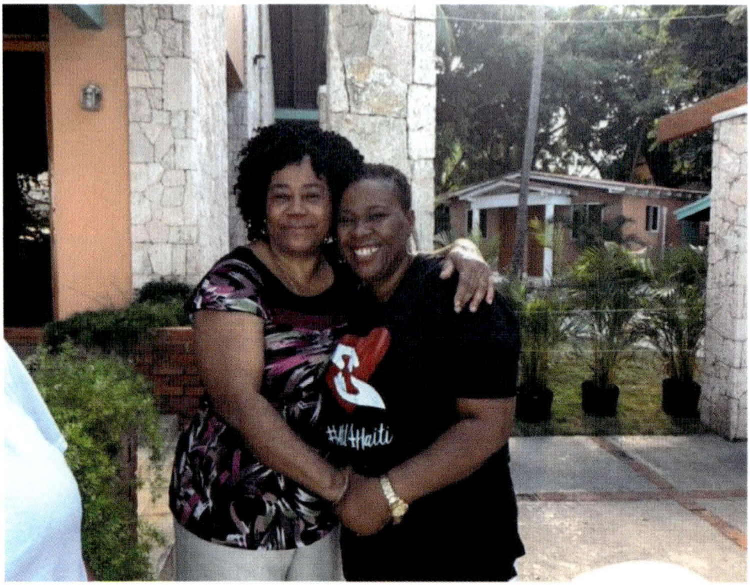
#All4Haiti

The Road to Purpose

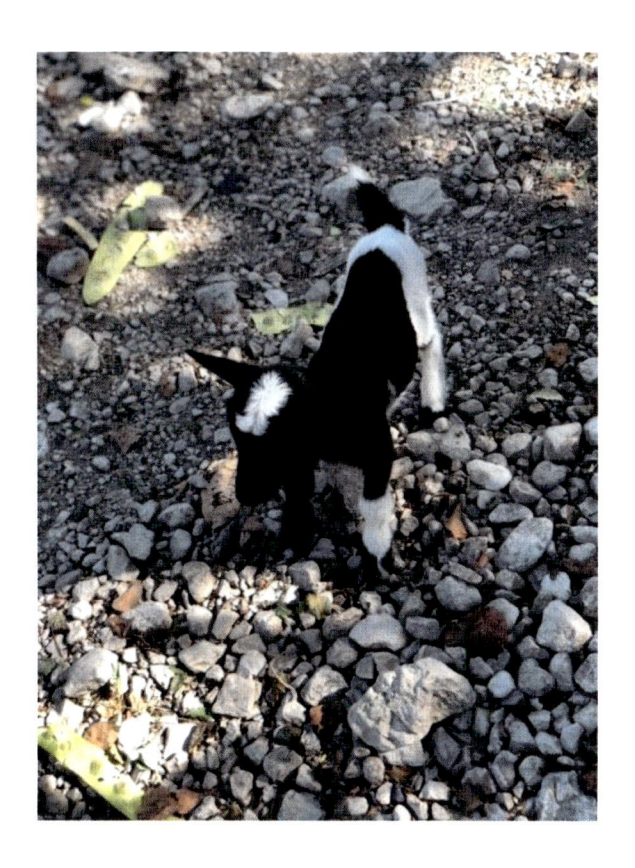

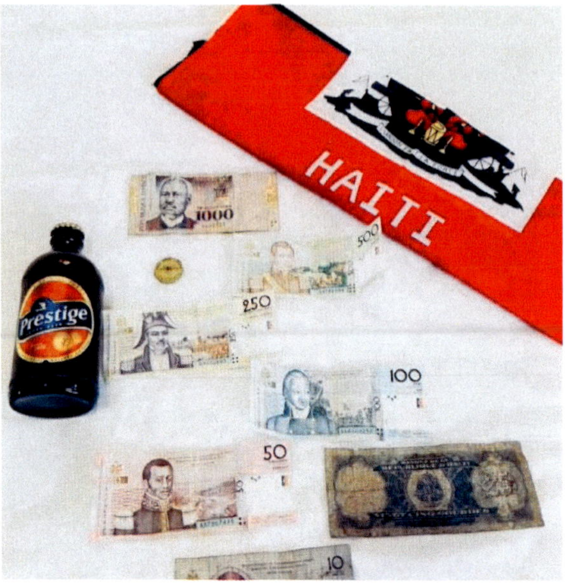
HAITI
Prestige
1000
500
250
100
50
10

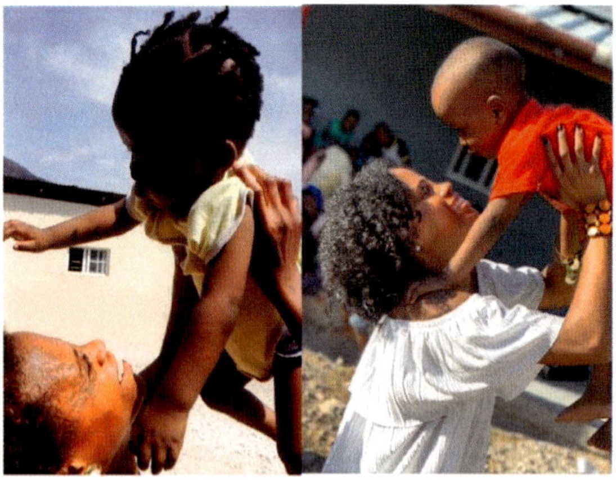

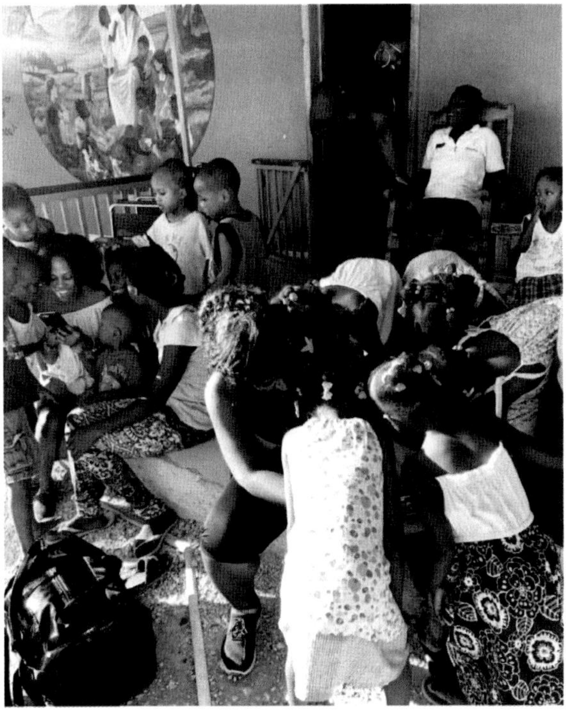

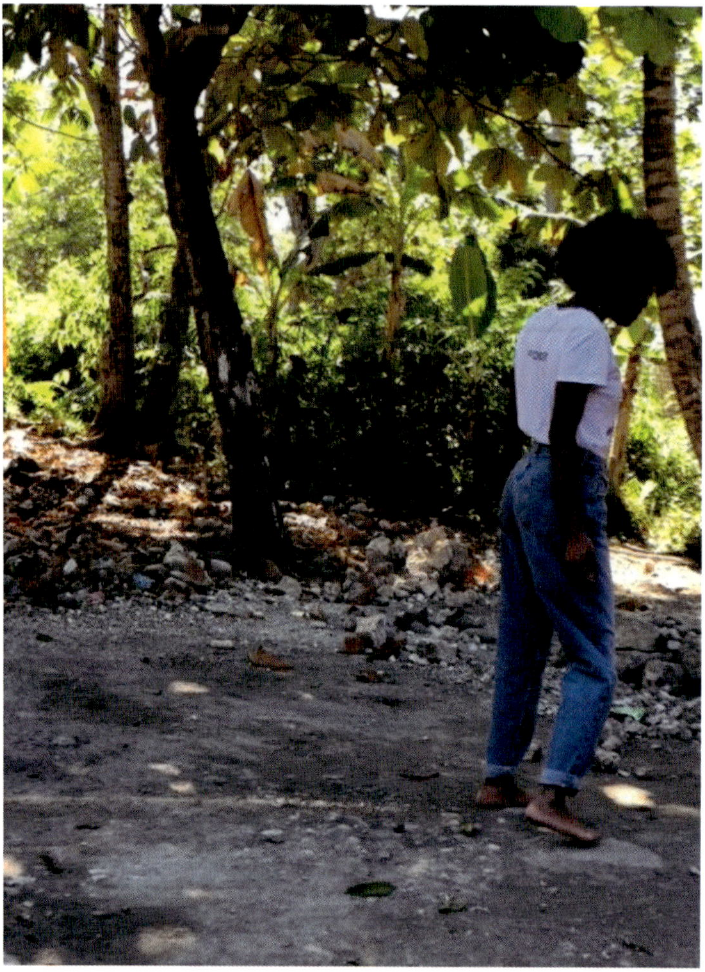

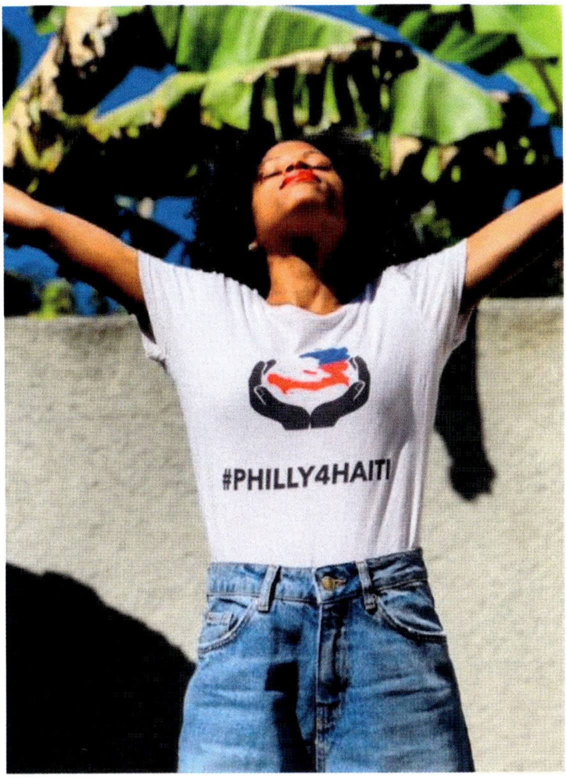
#PHILLY4HAITI

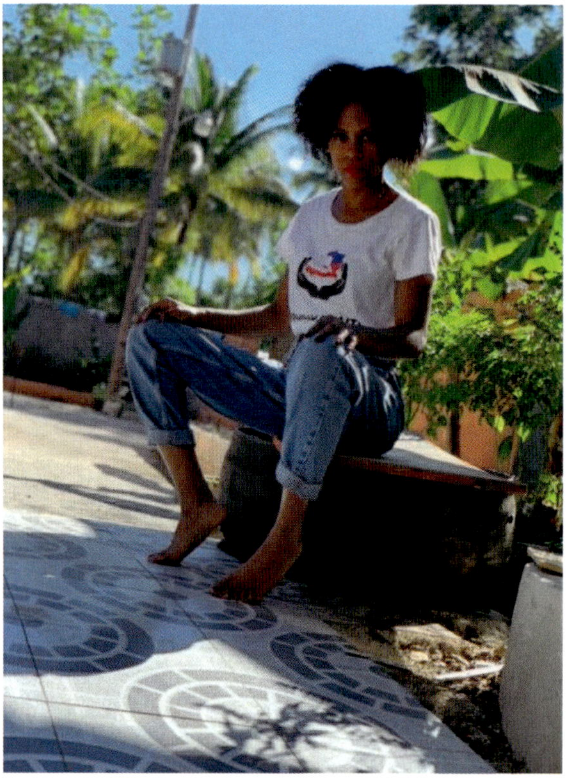

The Road to Purpose

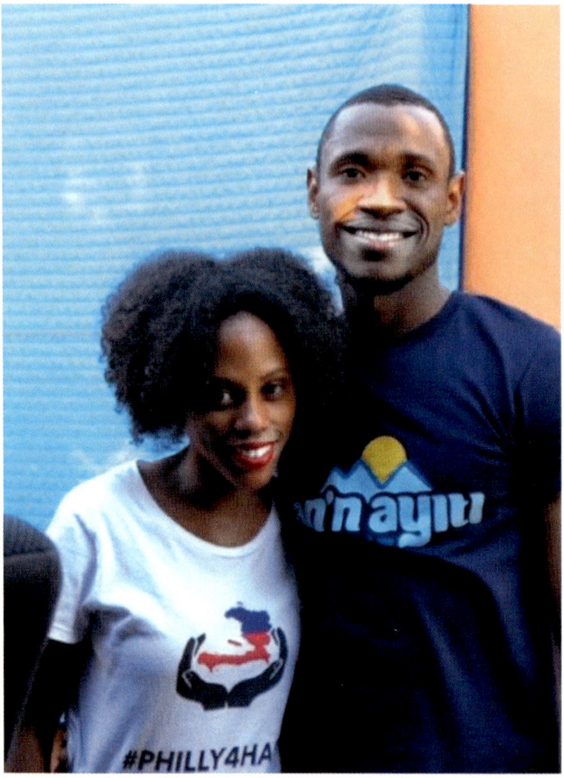
n'n ayiti
#PHILLY4HA

The Road to Purpose

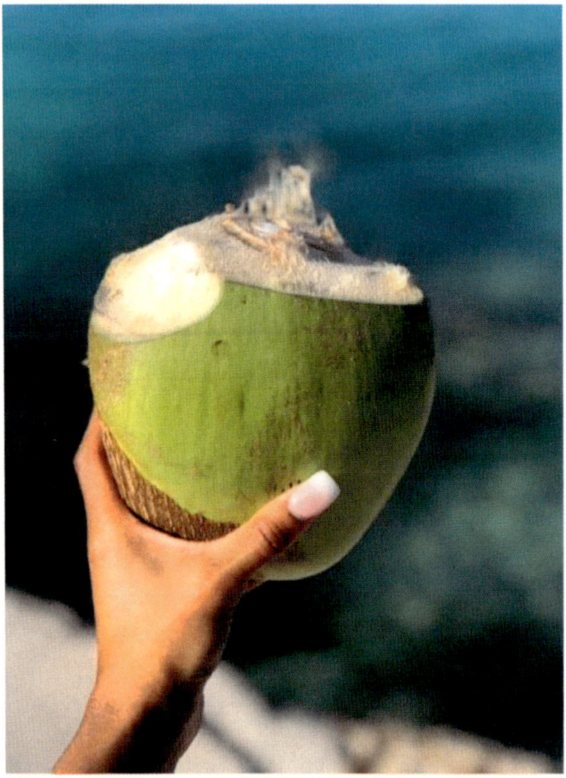

The Road to Purpose

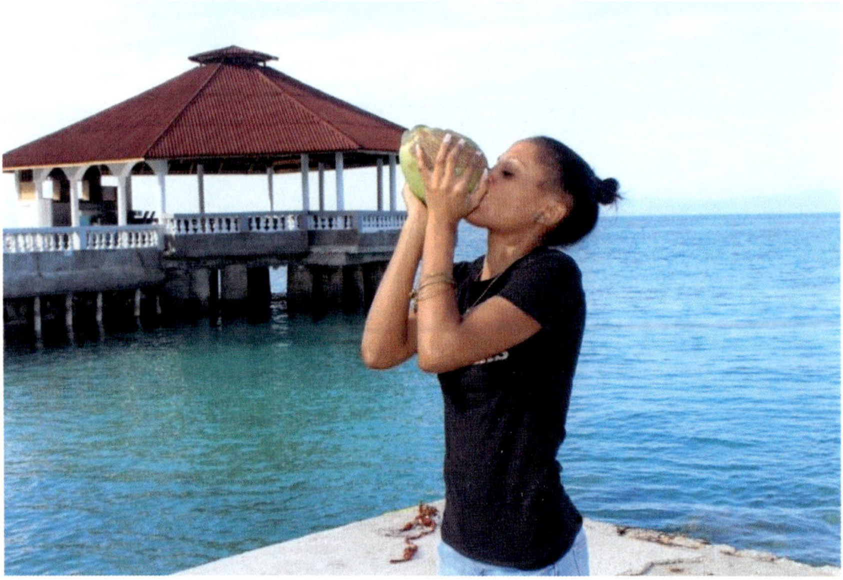

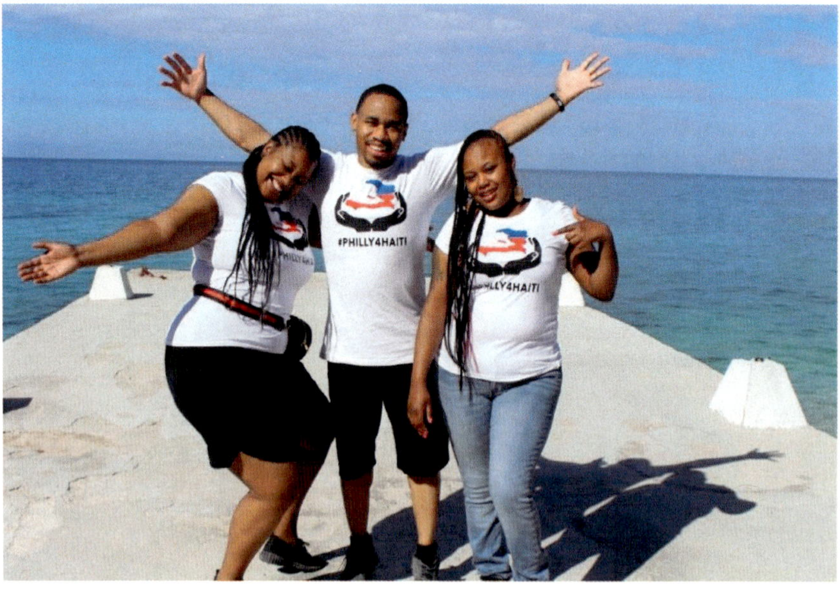
#PHILLY4HAITI

The Road to Purpose

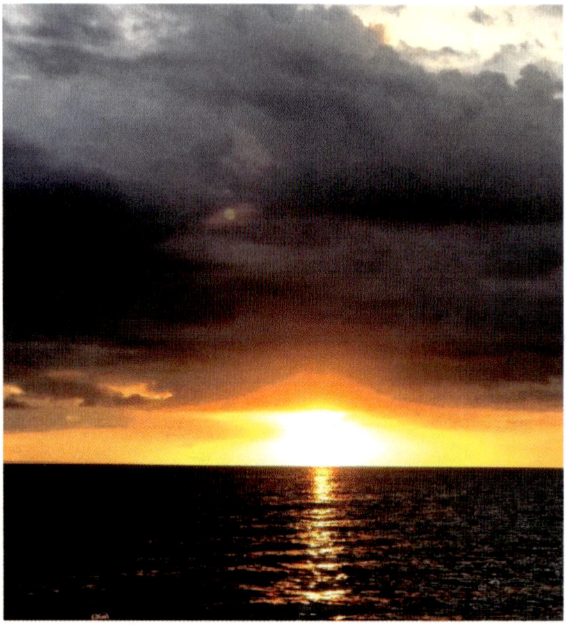

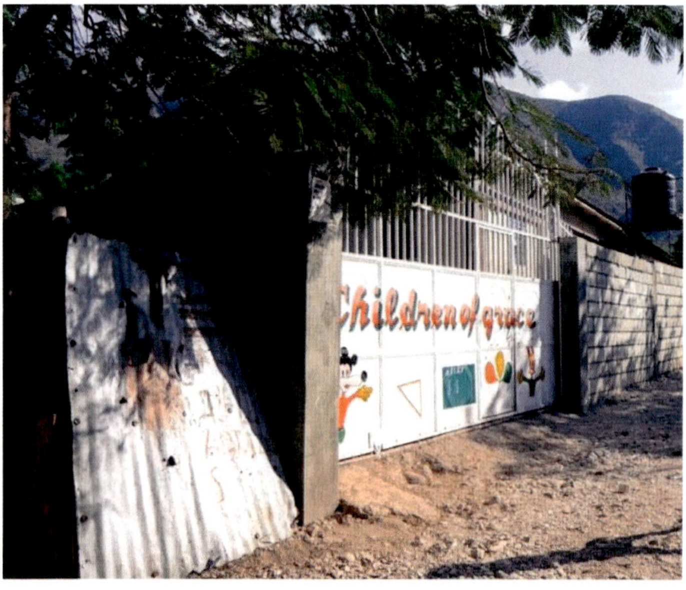
Children of grace

The Road to Purpose

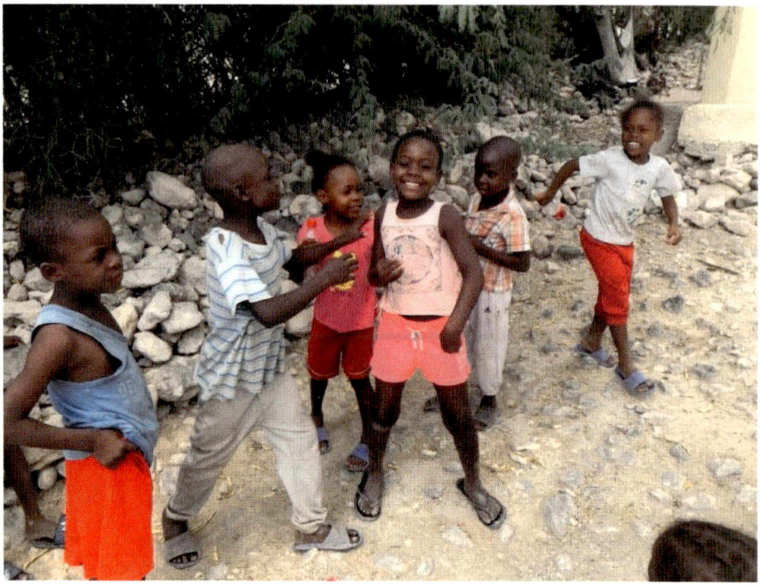

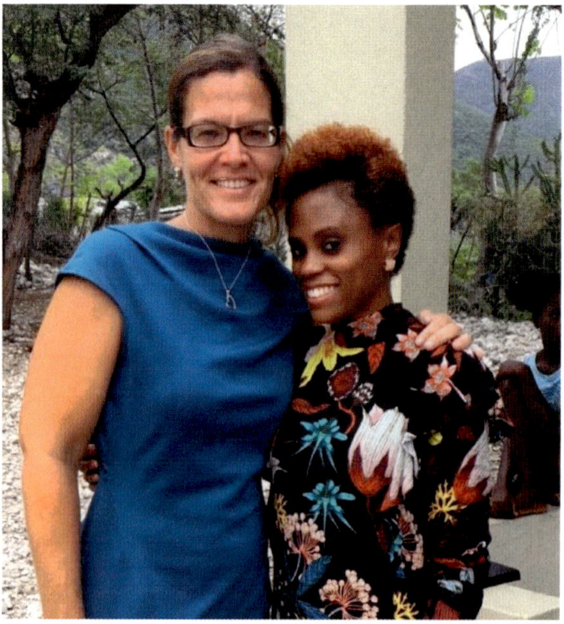

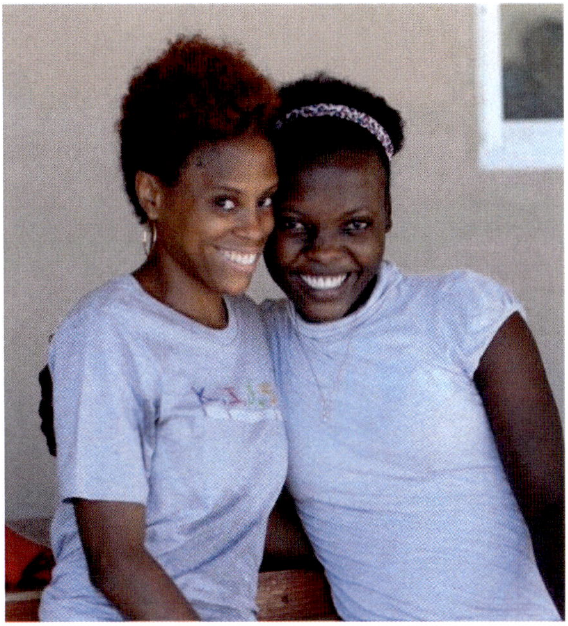

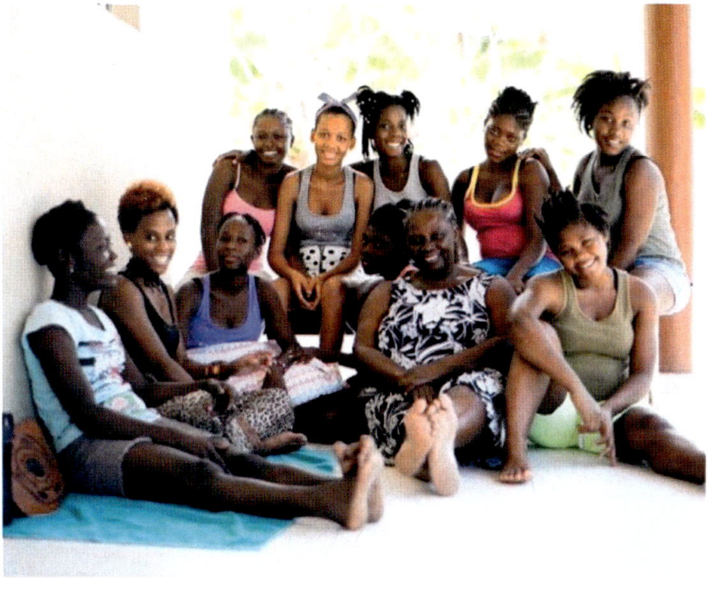

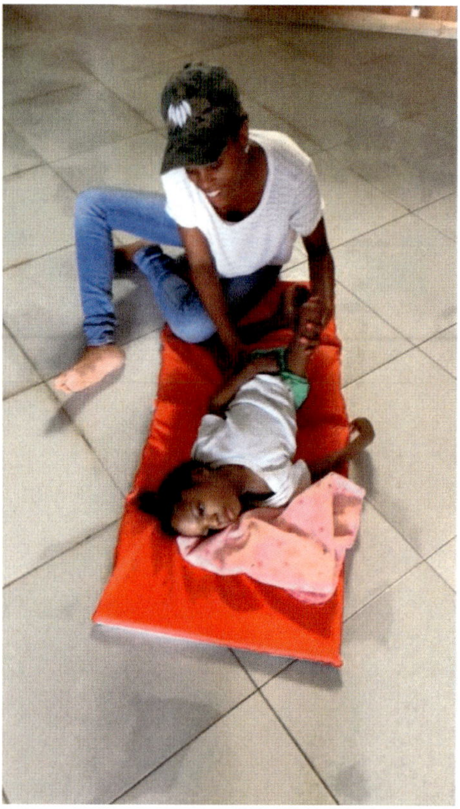

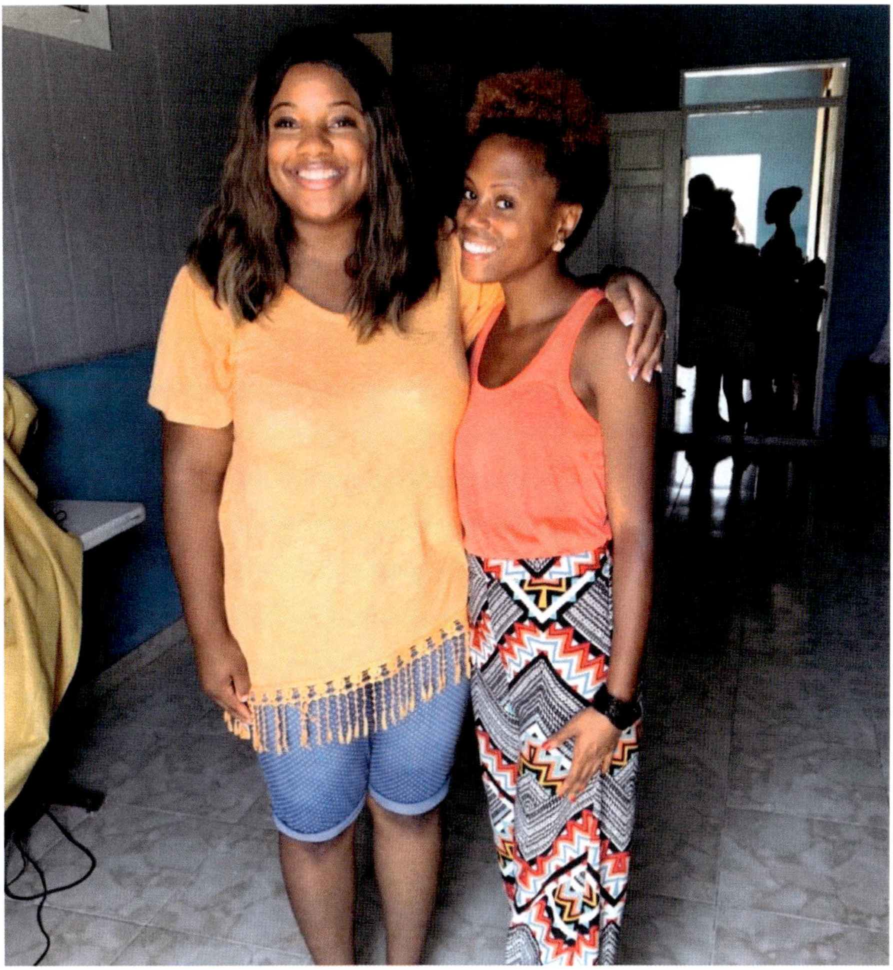

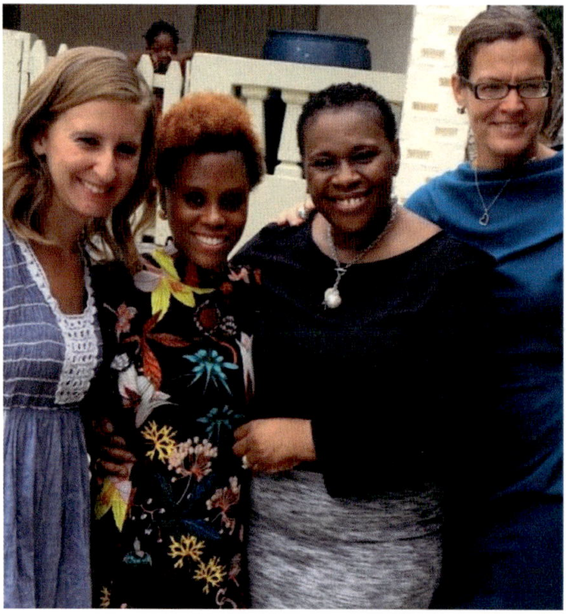

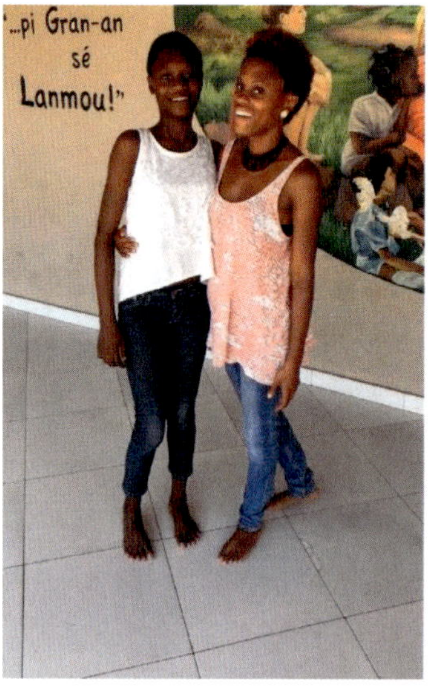
"...pi Gran-an
sé
Lanmou!"

The Road to Purpose

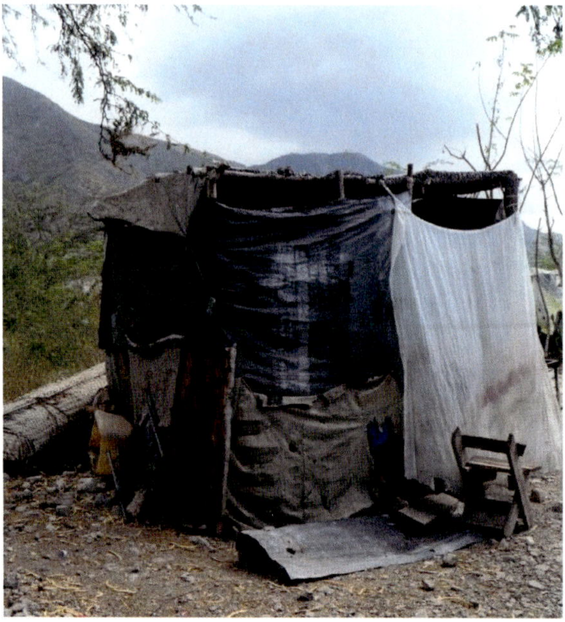

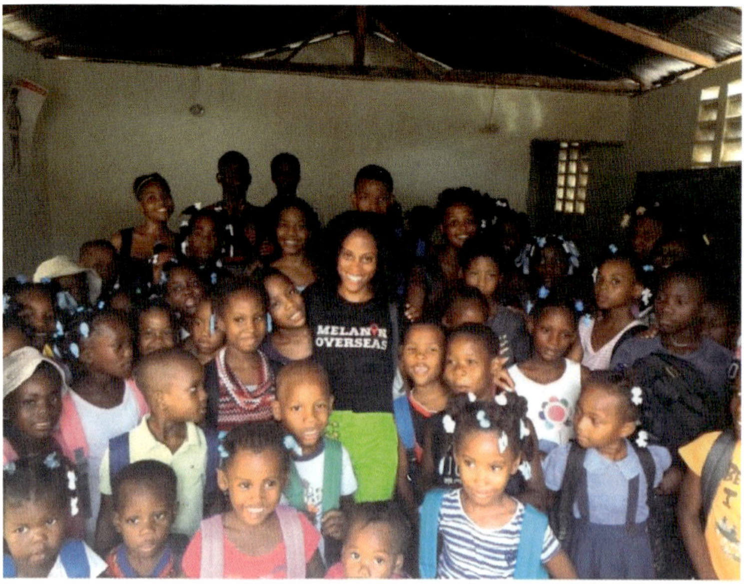
OVERSEAS

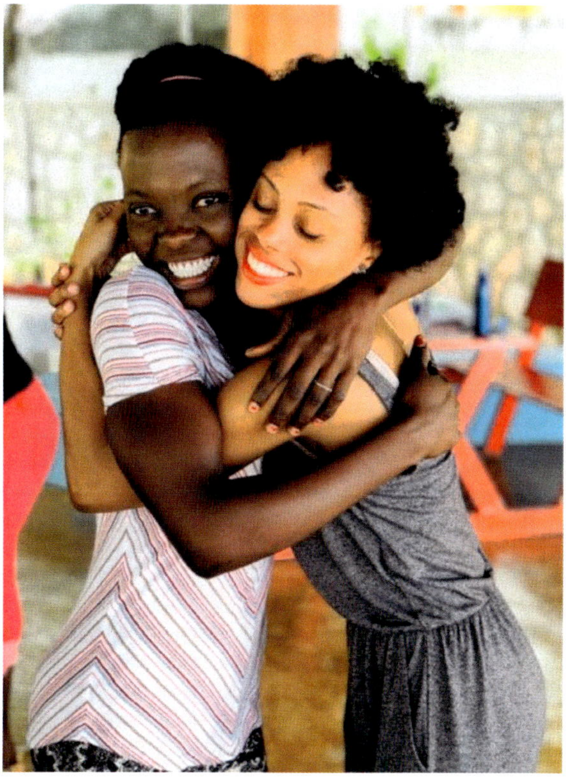

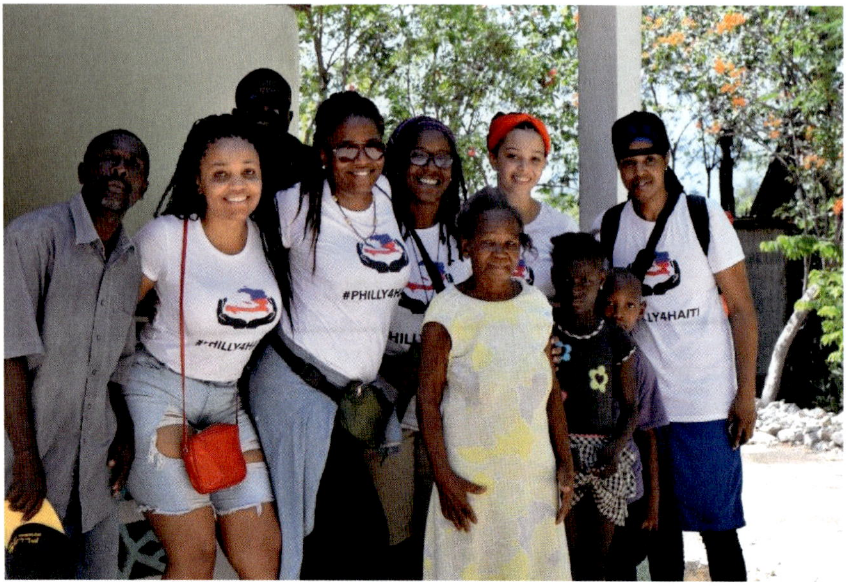

The Road to Purpose

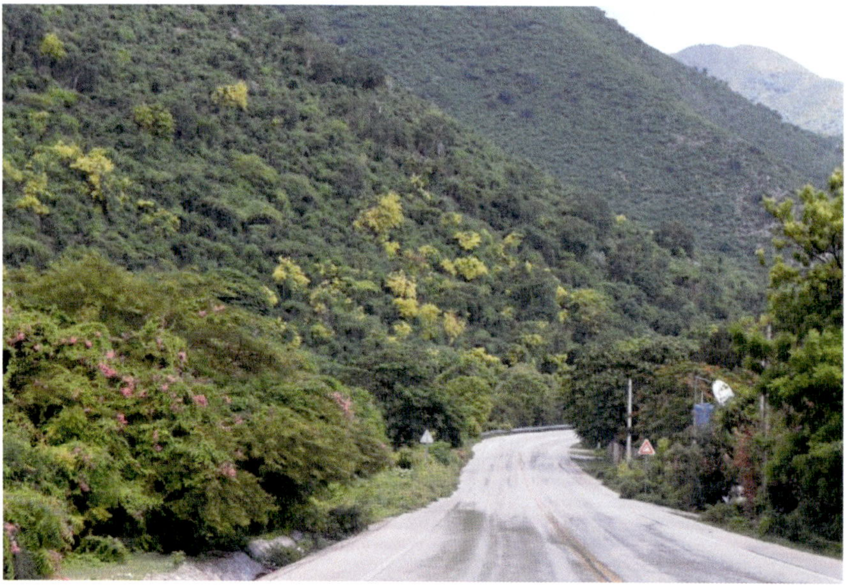

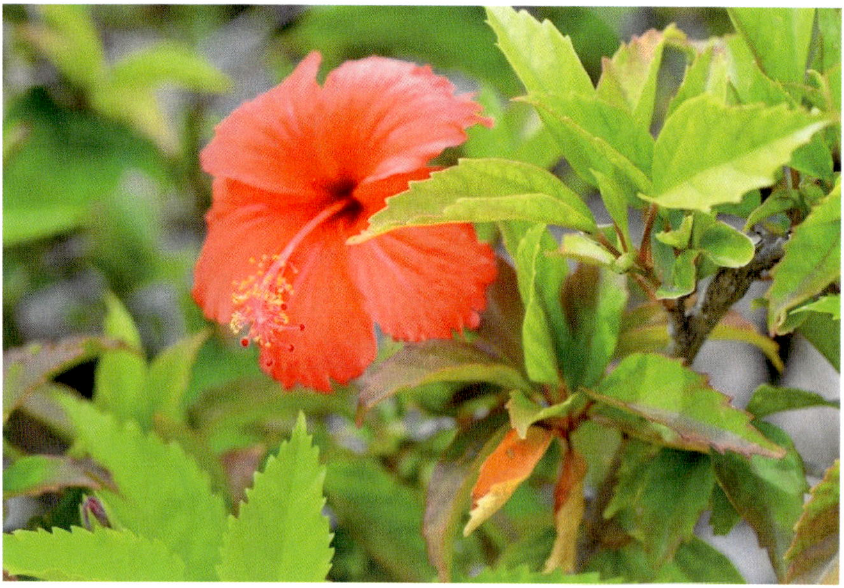

The Road to Purpose

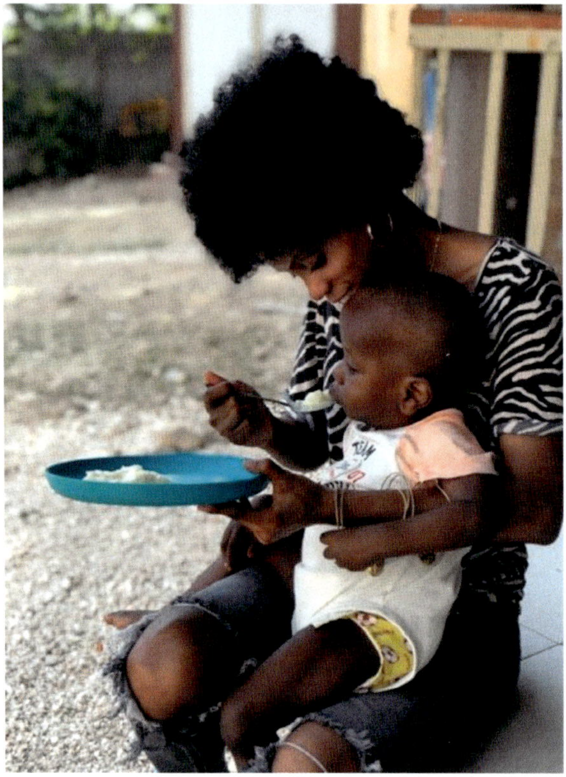

The Road to Purpose

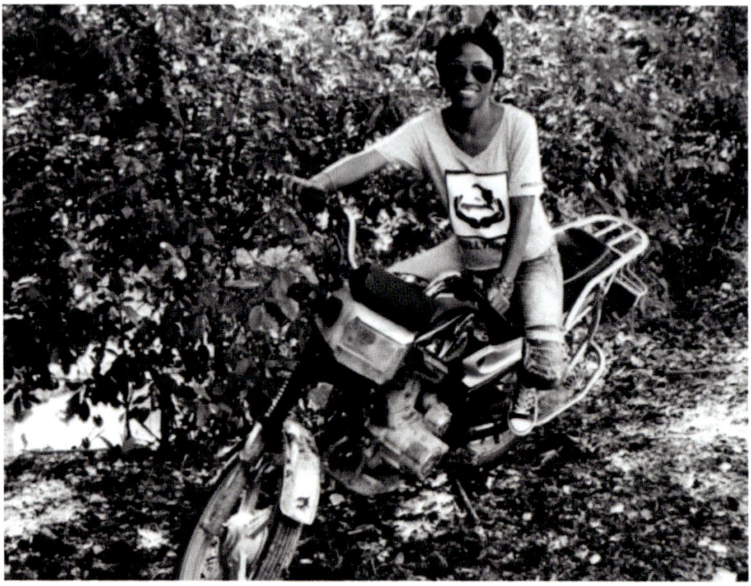

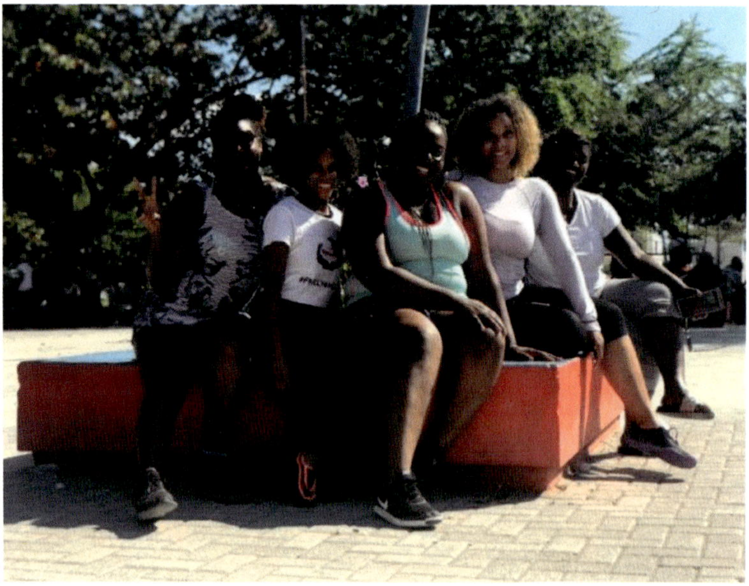

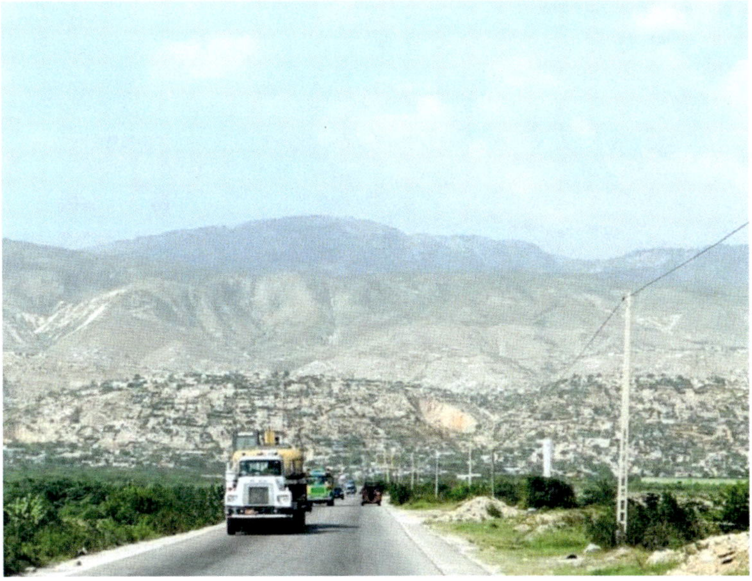

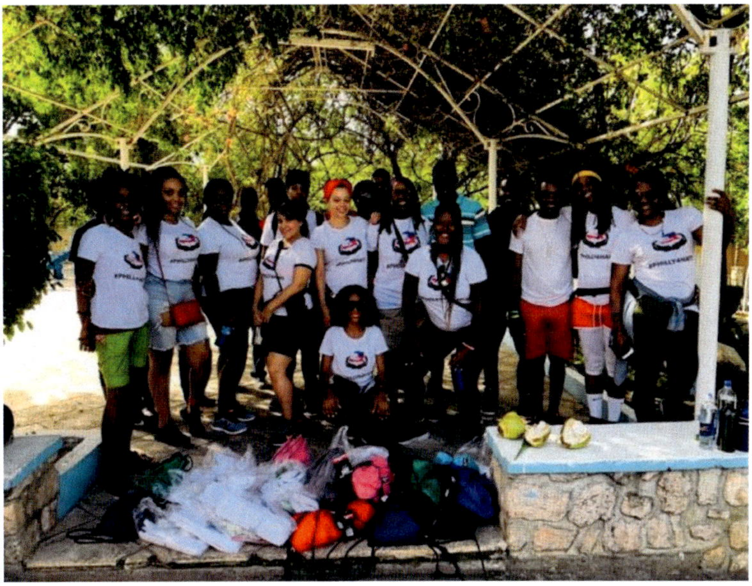

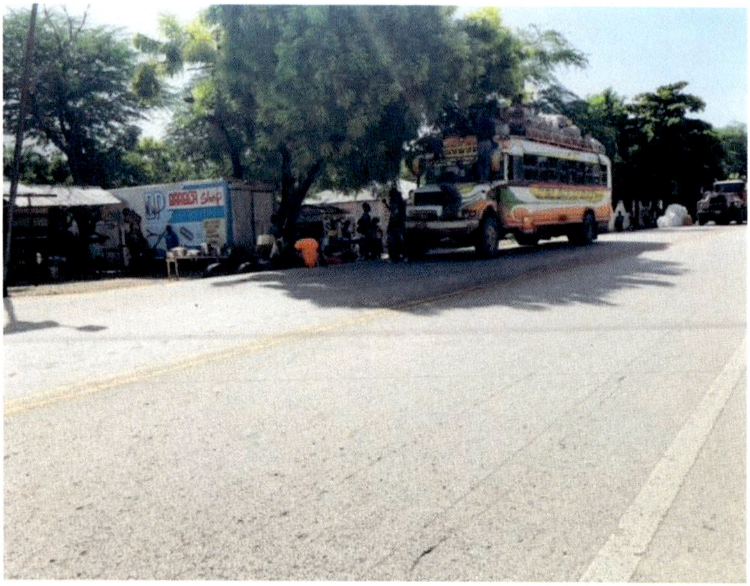

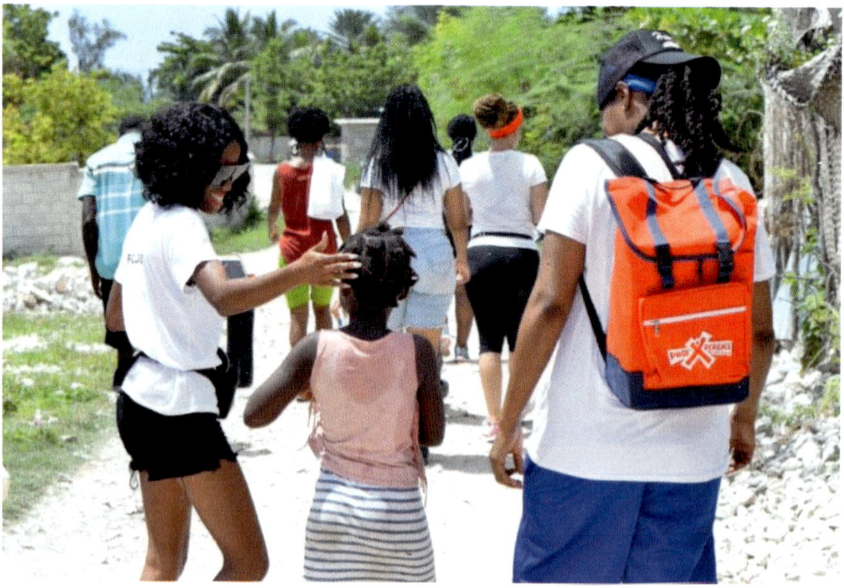

The Road to Purpose

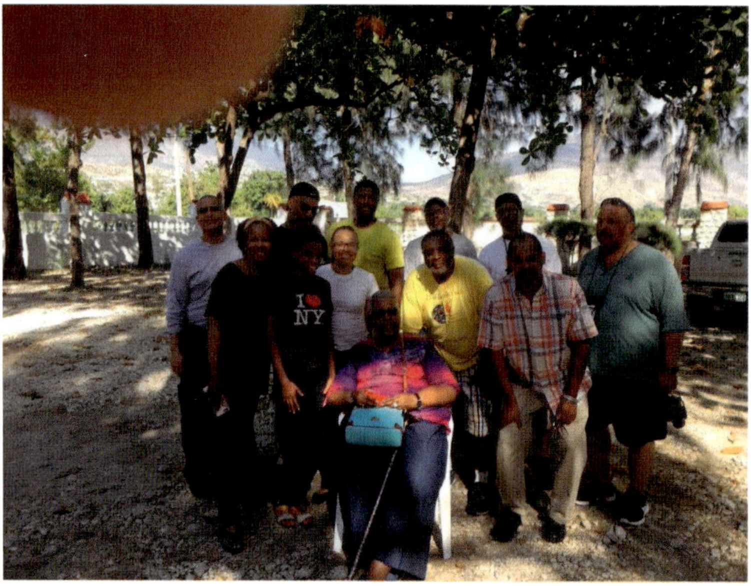
I ♥ NY

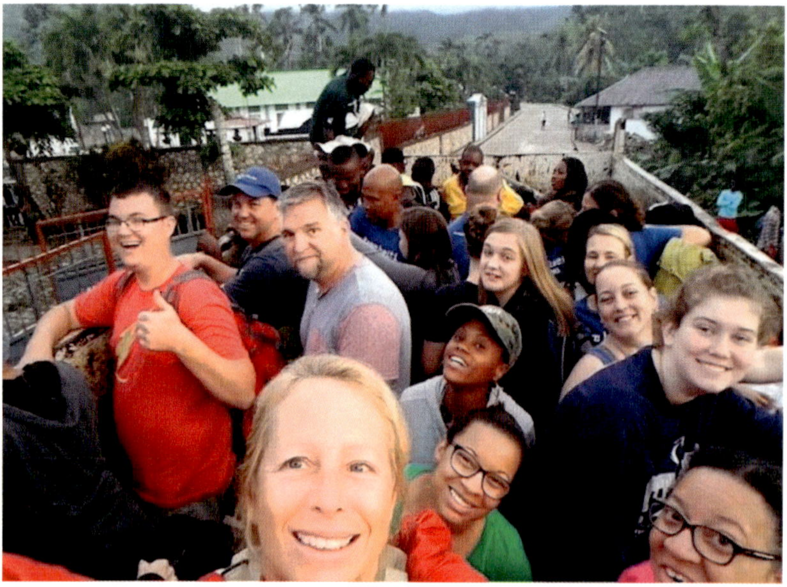

The Road to Purpose

Dear self,

You forget what you have done to be where you are, how hard you have worked, how difficult was the struggle to become who you are today, and the fire around you is consuming the fire inside of you.

Sometimes you just feel like you want to give up; you feel like no one can understand what you're going through. You feel like you are alone in the crowd and the only one to suffer like that in your environment, in it is exactly at this moment you should put in your mind that you're on a big mission, and once the dream is big the sacrifices will be also.

People will see what you are showing, People will see the results, good or bad, but they don't need to know all the issues that are inside of the great results they see as people always like to see the beauty of a brand new car but don't know anything about its engine.

We should always accept and wait for the personal challenges; it is what make us stronger. We should face challenges because they are the best teachers that can help us become better every day.

Carine Dorlus

ABOUT THE AUTHOR

Carine Dorlus is a Haitian-American born and raised in Philadelphia, Pennsylvania. She is passionate about helping children in her own community and from her parents' homeland. Carine is a motivational speaker and global human-philanthropist. Her most cherished attribute is impacting people's lives, each and every day! She is the true definition of what you call a LEADER!

Made in the
USA
Columbia, SC